A World without Agriculture

THE HENRY WENDT LECTURE SERIES

The Henry Wendt Lecture is delivered annually at the American Enterprise Institute by a scholar who has made major contributions to our understanding of the modern phenomenon of globalization and its consequences for social welfare, government policy, and the expansion of liberal political institutions. The lecture series is part of AEI's Wendt Program in Global Political Economy, established through the generosity of the SmithKline Beecham pharmaceutical company (now GlaxoSmithKline) and Mr. Henry Wendt, former chairman and chief executive officer of SmithKline Beecham and trustee emeritus of AEI.

A World without Agriculture

The Structural Transformation in Historical Perspective

C. Peter Timmer

The AEI Press

Publisher for the American Enterprise Institute

WASHINGTON, D.C.

Distributed to the Trade by National Book Network, 15200 NBN Way, Blue Ridge Summit, PA 17214. To order call toll free 1-800-462-6420 or 1-717-794-3800. For all other inquiries please contact the AEI Press, 1150 Seventeenth Street, N.W., Washington, D.C. 20036 or call 1-800-862-5801.

Library of Congress Cataloging-in-Publication Data

Timmer, C. Peter.
  A world without agriculture : the structural transformation in historical perspective / C. Peter Timmer.
      p. cm.
  Includes bibliographical references.
  ISBN-13: 978-0-8447-4279-3
  ISBN-10: 0-8447-4279-1
  1. Agriculture—Economic aspects—History. 2. Economic development—History. I. Title.

HD1415.T54 2009
338.1—dc22

2008053972

13 12 11 10 09   1 2 3 4 5

Printed in the United States of America

Contents

List of Illustrations

Acknowledgments

This essay relies heavily on my own teaching and research over the past several decades. Working Paper 150, plus its technical appendix, available at www.cgdev.org, provides more extensive discussion of the data and statistical details of the new empirical evidence (Timmer and Akkus 2008). I thank Ms. Selvin Akkus, who was a research assistant *extraordinaire* at the Center for Global Development from 2006 to 2008, for all her help and insights.

1

The Structural Transformation
in Historical Perspective

In early eighteenth-century France, the Physiocrats argued that all real income originated in agriculture. In rebutting that view in the early nineteenth century, David Ricardo's model of comparative advantage still relied on two agriculturally based products (wine and cloth) to demonstrate the gains from trade. In the early twentieth century, the co-inventor of modern national income accounts, Colin Clark, made agriculture the "primary" industry.[1]

From a historical perspective, it is impossible to imagine a world without agriculture. Just a hundred years ago, four out of five households in the world would have been engaged primarily in farming. Now, in rich countries, farmers are a tiny share of the workforce. Indeed, in the United States today there are more lawyers than farmers, more dry cleaning establishments than farms. The structural transformation is truly a radical force, and it is propelling the global economy toward "a world without agriculture" in an apparently inexorable manner. In figure 1-1 (page 7), the share of employment in agriculture and the share of agriculture in gross domestic product (GDP) are converging to—well, zero. Based on simple extrapolation of historical trends, the world's last farmer will sell his or her final crop sometime in the next century.

The juxtaposition of agriculture's historical importance with its apparent modern irrelevance presents a conundrum. A simple extrapolation of agriculture's declining share in national income is obviously wrong. In reality, the world produces more agricultural output than ever before. Farmers will still be growing food, fiber, and industrial raw materials centuries from now. But where? And

1

how much? And at what value? These are the questions that modern development economists—and policymakers in rich countries—must address if the world's poor countries are to achieve their full economic potential.

At one end of the spectrum, the *economies* of rich countries really do look as if their agricultural sectors have basically disappeared. But no external observer—not even the proverbial visitor from Mars—would believe that agriculture has disappeared based on the *politics* of rich countries. Politicians in nearly all countries of the Organisation for Economic Co-operation and Development (OECD) find it prudent to expend huge sums in subsidizing and protecting their farmers, often to the direct detriment of farmers in poor countries, and always to the detriment of their own taxpayers and consumers. Ending agriculture's special claim on public resources in rich countries would help rich and poor countries alike.

On the other hand, a world without agriculture is unimaginable for the 1.2 billion people who live on less than a dollar a day. Three-quarters of them depend directly or indirectly on agriculture for their livelihoods, and they will for decades to come. The paradox, of course, is that the people who most need investments (public and private) to raise their agricultural productivity are precisely the ones least likely to obtain them. The paradox has not gone unnoticed, but for more than two decades the development profession has been remarkably reluctant to face the issue squarely.

A "world without agriculture" would actually make life much easier for development agencies and for politicians in rich countries. "Getting agriculture moving" in poor countries is a complicated, long-run process that requires close, but flexible, relationships between the public and private sectors. Donor agencies are not good at this. More problematic, the process of agricultural development requires good economic governance in the countries themselves if it is to work rapidly and efficiently. Aid donors cannot hope to contribute good governance themselves—and they may well impede it.

Ever since the mid-1980s there has been serious discussion that major regions should pursue a development strategy that explicitly *rejects* a role for agriculture. These regions are still poor and depend in relative terms far more heavily on agriculture as a source of income than richer countries. But in a truly global economy with free trade, such a strategy has seemed theoretically possible. The theories suggest the emergence of developing regions of the world where all food and agricultural products come from international markets, and domestic agricultural sectors disappear.

This "world without agriculture" is not a vision of Singapore and Hong Kong, or the oil-rich countries of the Middle East. Rather, for many of the world's *poorest* countries, especially in Africa, a future without agriculture has been urged as the efficient path to development. Mark Rosenzweig, then the director of Harvard's Center for International Development, asked, "Should Africa do any agriculture at all?"[2] Adrian Wood, at the time chief economist for Britain's foreign aid agency, the Department for International Development (DfID), envisioned an Africa "hollowed out," with most of the population on the coasts where they could more effectively produce manufactured exports.[3] Many macroeconomists, convinced of the power of rapid economic growth to lift populations out of poverty, see resources devoted to slow-growing agriculture as wasted. A "pessimistic school" of agricultural development specialists thinks that, for both technical and economic reasons, Africa cannot rely on agriculture as a source of growth or poverty reduction.[4]

In a world of ample food supplies in global markets (some free as food aid) and increasingly open borders for trade, what is the role of agriculture in stimulating economic growth and connecting the poor to it? The question remains relevant in the face of the spike in prices for staple agricultural commodities seen in world markets early in 2008.[5] The answer to it—in political, economic, and technical terms—is the focus of the present study.

The Historical Perspective

Historically, the answer to the question about the role of agriculture in economic development is clear. No country has been able to sustain a rapid transition out of poverty without raising productivity in its agricultural sector (if it had one to start with—Singapore and

Hong Kong are, of course, exceptions). The process involves *a successful structural transformation* where agriculture, through higher productivity, provides food, labor, and even savings to the process of urbanization and industrialization. A dynamic agricultural sector raises labor productivity in the rural economy, pulls up wages, and gradually eliminates the worst dimensions of absolute poverty. Somewhat paradoxically, the process also leads to a decline in the relative importance of agriculture to the overall economy, as the industrial and service sectors grow even more rapidly, partly through stimulus from a modernizing agriculture and the migration of rural workers to urban jobs.

Despite this historical role of agriculture in economic development, both the academic and donor communities lost interest in the sector, starting in the mid-1980s, largely due to the low prices then prevailing in world markets for basic agricultural commodities. While a boon to poor consumers and a stimulus to labor-intensive growth, low prices made it hard to justify policy support for the agricultural sector, or new funding for agricultural research or commodity-oriented projects.[6] History lessons are a frail reed in the face of market realities (or, alternatively, if one is a development economist, in the face of general equilibrium models purportedly demonstrating a sharply declining role for agriculture in economic growth). But the "current realities" staring policymakers in the face are price trends, not the underlying mechanisms driving the structural transformation.

History lessons have a way of returning to haunt those who ignore them. This is especially true when the lessons are robust, have been observed for very long periods of time, and fit within a broader economic understanding of how farmers and consumers (and politicians) behave. The lessons from the structural transformation fit these conditions, and, as figure 1-1 (page 7) illustrates, they do point toward "a world without agriculture." We can translate these history lessons into an understanding of the connections between sectoral growth and reductions in poverty, and with this understanding will come insights into how to manage agricultural development to enhance both efficiency and equity.

The Structural Transformation

The structural transformation is the defining characteristic of the development process, both cause and effect of economic growth.[7] Four quite relentless and interrelated processes define the structural transformation: a declining share of agriculture in GDP and employment (see figure 1-1 on page 7); a rural-to-urban migration that stimulates the process of urbanization; the rise of a modern industrial and service economy; and a demographic transition from high rates of births and deaths (common in backward rural areas) to low rates of births and deaths (associated with better health standards in urban areas).

The final outcome of the structural transformation, already visible on the horizon in rich countries, is an economy and society where agriculture as an economic activity has no distinguishing characteristics from other sectors, at least in terms of the productivity of labor and capital. This stage also shows up in figure 1-1, as the gap in labor productivity between agricultural and nonagricultural workers approaches zero when incomes are high enough and the two sectors have been integrated by well-functioning labor and capital markets.

All societies want to raise the productivity of their economies. That is the only way to achieve and sustain higher standards of living. The mechanisms for doing so are well known in principle, if difficult to implement in practice. They include the utilization of improved technologies, investment in higher educational attainment and skill levels for the labor force, lower transactions costs (to help connect and integrate economic activities), and increased efficiency in the allocation of resources. The process of actually implementing these mechanisms over time is known as economic development. When successful, and sustained for decades, economic development leads to the structural transformation of the economy.

In the long run, the way to raise rural productivity is to raise urban productivity (or, as Chairman Mao crudely but correctly put it, "The only way out for agriculture is industry"). Unless the nonagricultural economy is growing, there is little long-run hope for agriculture. At the same time, the historical record is very clear on the key role played by agriculture itself in stimulating the nonagricultural economy.[8]

In the early stages of the structural transformation in all countries, there is a substantial gap between the share of the labor force employed in agriculture and the share of GDP generated by that labor force. Figure 1-1 shows that this gap narrows with higher incomes. This convergence is also part of the structural transformation, reflecting better-integrated labor and financial markets. The role of better technology and higher productivity *on farms* as a way to raise incomes in agriculture is controversial. Most of the evidence suggests that gains in farm productivity have been quickly lost (to farmers) in lower prices and that income convergence between agriculture and nonagriculture is driven primarily by the labor market.[9]

Moreover, in many countries, this structural gap actually widens during periods of rapid growth, as was evident in even the earliest developers, the now-rich OECD countries. When overall GDP is growing rapidly, the share of agriculture in GDP falls much faster than the share of agricultural labor in the overall labor force. The turning point in the gap generated by these differential processes, after which labor productivity in the two sectors begins to converge, has also been moving "to the right" over time, requiring progressively higher per-capita incomes before the convergence process begins.

This lag inevitably presents political problems as farm incomes visibly fall behind incomes being earned in the rest of the economy. The long-run answer, of course, is faster integration of farm labor into the nonfarm economy (including the rural nonfarm economy), but the historical record shows that such integration takes a long time. It was not fully achieved in the United States until the 1980s,[10] and evidence presented here suggests the productivity gap is becoming increasingly difficult to bridge through economic growth alone. *This lag in real earnings from agriculture is the fundamental cause of the deep political tensions generated by the structural transformation, and it is growing more extreme.* Historically, the completely uniform response to these political tensions has been to protect the agricultural sector from international competition and, ultimately, to provide direct income subsidies to farmers.[11] We now

FIGURE 1-1

THE STRUCTURAL TRANSFORMATION IN EIGHTY-SIX COUNTRIES FROM 1965 TO 2000

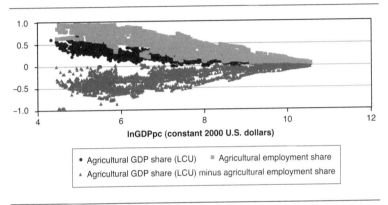

SOURCE: Timmer and Akkus 2008.

NOTE: Figure 1-1 shows the declining share of agriculture in employment (squares), in economic output (circles), and the gap between these two shares (triangles), as per capita incomes increase.

understand that the political economy of this process is driven by the structural transformation itself.

The Structural Transformation as a General Equilibrium Process

The economic and political difficulties encountered during a rapid structural transformation are illustrated schematically in figure 1-2, which shows a representative structural transformation, and numerically in table 1-1, which presents the simple mathematics of structural change over a twenty-year period of economic growth and transformation. Although figure 1-2 (page 9) shows the share of agricultural labor in the total labor force and the contribution of agriculture to overall GDP both declining smoothly until parity is reached when a country is "rich," the actual relationship between the two shares depends critically on the pace of change *outside* of agriculture—and on the labor intensity of those activities.

Figure 1-2 also shows a basic fact that is often overlooked in political discussions about the "failure" of agriculture to grow as fast as the rest of the economy, and thus to decline as a share of GDP and in the labor force: Despite the structural transformation, *agricultural output continues to rise in absolute value*. Even as the number of farmers falls toward zero, total farm output sets new records.[12] That is what rising productivity is all about!

Table 1-1 illustrates the impact of three alternative paths for a country's structural transformation. At the starting point, industry, services, and agriculture contribute 20, 30, and 50 percent to GDP, respectively, and the share of workers in each sector is 9.7, 20.8, and 69.5 percent, respectively—fairly typical for a country in the very early stages of development. Labor productivity in each sector is 3, 2, and 1 units of output per worker per year, respectively, so overall labor productivity for the entire economy is the weighted average, or 1.4.

The economy then grows for twenty years, with industry growing 7.5 percent per year, services 5.0 percent per year, and agriculture 3.0 percent per year. The overall rate of growth at the start is 4.5 percent per year. These growth rates result from technological change that is sector-specific on the supply side, and from differential demand patterns that reflect Engel's Law (the share of food in consumers' budgets declines as incomes rise). The *trade implications* of these differential growth rates, which are representative of long-run rates seen in successful developing countries, are not shown in table 1-1; but the economy must be relatively open to trade to sustain such rates.

The "simple mathematics" of the structural transformation show what happens to the economy and to labor productivity through twenty years of reasonably rapid growth. At an aggregate level, total GDP grows from 100 to 255, an annual growth rate of 4.8 percent per year. Notice the acceleration in the growth rate despite the assumption that each sector grows at a constant rate for twenty years, a result of changing sectoral weights. Indeed, GDP growth in the last year of the exercise is 5.2 percent, compared with just 4.5 percent per year at the start, despite the fact that each sector continues

FIGURE 1-2

TRENDS IN AGRICULTURAL OUTPUT DURING THE COURSE OF THE STRUCTURAL TRANSFORMATION FROM "POOR" TO "RICH"

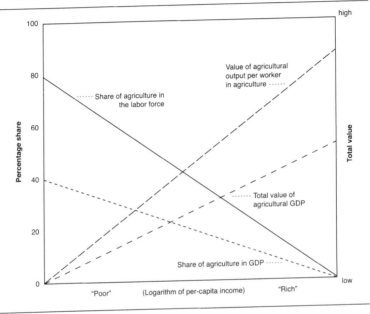

SOURCE: Author's diagram.
NOTE: There is no significance to the location of the crossing of the solid and dashed lines in this schematic diagram.

to grow at a constant rate. If the labor force grows by 2.0 percent per year during this exercise, labor productivity in aggregate will grow to 2.4 (from 1.4 in the base year), a healthy growth rate of 2.7 percent per year.

But the critical story is at the sectoral level, where the structural transformation becomes visible. Table 1-1 shows three possible growth paths that encompass modern development experience. Path A follows the basic logic of the Lewis model of economic development, which uses surplus labor in the agricultural sector to fuel labor-intensive industrialization.[13] This path holds labor productivity *constant* in the industrial and service sectors, as they absorb labor

TABLE 1-1

THE SIMPLE (BUT IMPLACABLE) MATHEMATICS
OF THE STRUCTURAL TRANSFORMATION
(Output measured in "real" units of domestic currency per year)

Start (Year 0)	Industry	Services	Agriculture	GDP
Output	20	30	50	100
Share of GDP	20	30	50	100
Number of workers[a]	7	15	50	72
Labor productivity	3	2	1	1.4
Share of workers in total	9.7	20.8	69.5	100
Sectoral growth rates (%/year)	7.5	5.0	3.0	4.5
Contribution to growth in year 1	1.5	1.5	1.5	4.5

End (Year 20)	Industry	Services	Agriculture	GDP
Output	85	80	90	255
Share of GDP	33.3	31.4	35.3	100
Number of workers[b]				
Path A	28	40	39	107
Path B	14	24	69	107
Path C	7	15	85	107
Labor productivity				
Path A	3	2	2.32	2.4
Path B	6.3	3.3	1.31	2.4
Path C	12.7	5.3	1.06	2.4
Share of workers in total				
Path A	26.2	37.4	36.4	100
Path B	13.1	22.4	64.5	100
Path C	6.5	14.0	79.5	100
Contribution to growth in year 20	2.5	1.6	1.1	5.2

continued on the next page

Table 1-1, continued from the previous page

Ratio of labor productivity (wages or income) in the top quintile of workers relative to the bottom quintile

Start	2.55
Path A	1.50
Path B	4.02
Path C	7.27

SOURCE: Author's calculations.

NOTES: a. The active labor force will grow by 2.0 percent per year; b. Path A assumes that labor productivity in industry and services remains *constant* as the two sectors absorb new laborers at the same rate as output expansion (the classic Lewis assumption). Agricultural employment remains the residual, with changes there consistent with general equilibrium. In path B, labor productivity in industry and services increases at half the rate of output. In path C, labor productivity in the industrial and services sectors increases at the same rate as sectoral output, so no new labor is hired. Note that paths A and C are extremes that are somewhat outside historical experience.

from the agricultural sector at the same rates as each sector itself expands. The "Lewis path" of industrial and service growth leads to the fastest structural transformation of the three scenarios, and is so successful in pulling "surplus" labor out of agriculture that labor productivity in this sector is actually higher at the end than in the service sector, and only 23 percent less than in the industrial sector. No country has actually managed a growth path with quite that much labor intensity, although the East Asian experience has come closest. The structural transformation is extremely rapid with this path, and the *absolute* number of workers in agriculture is already declining after twenty years of rapid growth.

Path C lies at the opposite extreme, where labor productivity in the industrial and service sectors grows at the same rate as the sectors themselves. Thus, neither sector absorbs any new workers at all, so the entire increase in the labor force remains in agriculture. Because agricultural GDP is still rising faster than the labor force, labor productivity in the sector does rise slightly, but at only 0.3 percent per year. This pattern is closer to the African experience, although Indonesia in the 1950s and early 1960s looked similar. Not only is the absolute number of workers in agriculture still rising on this path; so, too, is the *share* of agricultural labor in the total labor force.

Path B is halfway between these two extremes, with labor productivity in the industrial and service sectors growing at half the rate of increase in sectoral output. The result is actually quite like the Indonesian experience since 1970. The agricultural labor force continues to rise (to 69, from 50 at the beginning) but is clearly near its peak—ten more years of such growth would see the agricultural labor force in absolute decline. Labor productivity in agriculture increases by 1.4 percent per year over the entire period, somewhat less than the rate found by Fuglie[14] for Indonesia from 1961 to 2000, the years of both rapid and slow growth in productivity.

But even this successful pattern of structural transformation leaves a serious problem for policymakers. As table 1-1 also shows, income distribution widens under this scenario, at least as measured by the ratio of labor productivity (wages) in the top quintile of laborers to that in the bottom quintile. From a starting ratio of 2.55, even path B yields a ratio of 4.02. Of course, things could be worse. If output expansion in industry and services does not employ new workers (path C), the ratio widens to 7.27! Only a pure "Lewis-style" pattern of growth (path A) narrows the distribution of labor income.

The point of this exercise is to emphasize the power, the inevitability, and the paradoxical nature of the structural transformation. Even a narrow focus on agricultural productivity per se must be set within this transformation. The crucial point is that the *faster* the structural transformation, the *faster* the decline in the share of agriculture in both the economy and the overall labor force. And the paradox is that the *faster* the structural transformation, the faster that rural productivity—proxied by rural labor productivity—*rises* (as in scenario A). *This is true even though the rate of growth of agricultural GDP is the same in all three scenarios.* Consequently, a broader focus on rural productivity and pathways out of rural poverty will inevitably incorporate the structural transformation as the basic framework for macro consistency and general equilibrium.

2

Common Patterns and Divergent Policies, 1965–2000

The empirics of the structural transformation have been a research topic for quite some time, as Syrquin notes:

> Modern analyses of sectoral transformation originated with Fisher (1935, 1939) and Clark (1940), and dealt with sectoral shifts in the composition of the labor force. As in most areas in economics one can find precursors of their ideas in earlier writings [by Sir William Petty and Friedrich List]. However, they were probably the first to deal with the process of reallocation during the epoch of modern economic growth, and to use the form of sectoral division (primary-secondary-tertiary) which, in one way or another, is still with us today.[1]

Kuznets provided the historical empirics and conceptual framework for modern analysis of the structural transformation, although he used no econometric techniques himself.[2] The first quantitative analyses of patterns in the transformation process were by Chenery and his collaborators.[3] The first systematic effort to study the evolution of the structural gap between labor productivity in agriculture and the rest of the economy was by van der Meer and Yamada in their analysis of productivity differences in Dutch and Japanese agriculture.[4]

Much effort has gone into finding "patterns of growth," especially for various typologies of countries. The earliest was the classification by Chenery and Taylor of their sample of countries into large, small-primary-oriented, and small-industry-oriented.[5] The goal has been to translate growth patterns in different typologies into strategies for development, but the uniqueness of country circumstances, especially in terms of political economy, has largely thwarted that effort. This study revives that search by bringing directly into the analysis the pressures on political economy from the structural transformation itself.

For the analysis below, eighty-six countries are followed from 1965 to 2000.[6] Empirically, most countries lie close to the average paths for the three variables of interest when year-specific and country-specific dummy variables are included along with the "standard" explanatory variables: logarithm of GDP per capita (lnGDPpc, where GDP per capita is measured in "real" U.S. dollars deflated to the year 2000 and converted at market exchange rates); lnGDPpc squared; and the agricultural to nonagricultural terms of trade (AgToT; see figure 1-1 and table 2-1 in this monograph). That is, all countries follow a variant of the basic structural transformation if their economies are growing. The three variables to be explained are

- the share of agricultural employment in total employment (AgEMPshr);

- the share of agricultural GDP in total GDP (AgGDPshr); and

- the difference between these two shares (AgGDPshr minus AgEMPshr equals AgGAPshr).

The Basic Patterns

Even the simplest specification for testing the relationship between share of agricultural employment in total employment—regression A-1 in table 2-1—explains 87 percent of the variance in the full sample of data.[7] The quadratic equation has the expected shape, with the linear term negative and the quadratic term positive.[8] Adding year and country coefficients (regression A-3) sharply reduces the size and statistical significance of both income terms.

TABLE 2-1

REGRESSIONS THAT EXPLAIN THE CHANGING ROLE OF
AGRICULTURAL WORKERS IN THE OVERALL LABOR FORCE
DURING THE STRUCTURAL TRANSFORMATION, 1965–2000

Regression number[a]	Dependent variable: Share of agricultural employment in total			
	A-1	A-2	A-3	A-4
Constant	2.227 (47.9)	2.351 (51.4)	0.962 (18.6)	0.745 (13.5)
lnGDPpc	–0.321 (25.2)	–0.342 (28.2)	–0.107 (8.0)	–0.0368 (2.5)
(lnGDPpc)sq.	0.0103 (12.3)	0.0118 (14.7)	0.00543 (5.9)	0.000617 (0.6)
Terms of trade				–0.000128 (7.1)
Year?	N	Y	Y	Y
Country?	N	N	Y	Y
Adj. Rsq	0.8694	0.8830	0.9851	0.9862
Turning point lnGDPpc GDPpc ($2,000)	15.582 $5.9M	14.492 $2.0M	9.853 $19,009	29.822 $8.9B (!)

Regression of country effects from regression A-3 on lnGDPpc2000

1.048   –0.130* lnGDPpc2000   Adj. Rsq 0.8463
(22.6)   (21.5)

Regression of year effects from regression A-3 on "Year" and "Year squared"

0.532   –0.0100* "Year" + 0.0000294* "Year"sq   Adj. Rsq 0.9996
(39.6)   (30.8)   (15.0)

SOURCE: Timmer and Akkus 2008, technical annex.
NOTES: a = t– statistics are in parentheses. "Year" = actual year minus 1900. The explanatory variables are logarithm of GDP per capita (lnGDPpc, where GDP per capita is measured in "real" U.S. dollars deflated to the year 2000 and converted at market exchange rates); lnGDPpc squared; and the agricultural to nonagricultural terms of trade (AgToT). The variable to be explained is the share of agricultural employment in total employment (AgEMPshr).

Finally, adding the agricultural to nonagricultural terms of trade (AgToT) calculated from the sectoral GDP deflators in national income accounts data—which is an index equal to one for all countries in 2000—further reduces the size and statistical significance of both income terms; the quadratic term is no longer significant. With this "full specification," the agricultural employment share approaches zero in a slow and linear fashion.

Turning now to the year and country effects,[9] we find that the year coefficients provide a smooth and large annual reduction in the share of employment in agriculture—1 percent per year. A slight but statistically significant quadratic term gradually offsets this negative time trend in the employment share. The negative trend provides an *exogenous source of convergence toward zero in the employment share*, independent of any relationship with per-capita incomes. These negative year coefficients suggest that technical change is an independent force in the structural transformation, above and beyond the impact of Engel's Law, which, as mentioned earlier, holds that the share of food expenditures in household budgets declines as household incomes increase.[10] A further implication is that, on average, this negative time effect causes labor productivity in agriculture to rise faster than in other sectors. The exogenous time effects mean that labor reallocation is also taking place independently of per-capita incomes, not just along with higher incomes. As already noted, this dimension of differential productivity growth is a normal feature of the structural transformation, widespread policy concerns about lagging incomes in the agricultural sector notwithstanding.

The separate intercept terms for each country from regression A-3 (the "country effects" in statistical terms) also exhibit a regular pattern: They are negatively, and significantly, related to the country's per-capita income in 2000. This relationship suggests that as they get richer, countries find a way to reduce the share of workers in agriculture independent of the structural reduction from the growth process itself. Political mechanisms would seem necessary to explain such a pattern. These results may reflect the response of political forces to the widening per-capita income difference

TABLE 2-2
REGRESSIONS THAT EXPLAIN THE CHANGING ROLE
OF AGRICULTURE IN GDP DURING THE STRUCTURAL
TRANSFORMATION, 1965–2000

Regression number[a]	Dependent variable: Share of agricultural GDP in total GDP			
	B-1	B-2	B-3	B-4
Constant	1.485 (45.5)	1.571 (47.2)	1.519 (20.9)	1.756 (26.9)
lnGDPpc	−0.273 (30.4)	−0.286 (32.8)	−0.292 (15.3)	−0.392 (22.5)
(lnGDPpc)sq.	0.0129 (21.7)	0.0138 (23.9)	0.0142 (10.7)	0.0215 (17.7)
Terms of trade				0.000648 (30.6)
Year?	N	Y	Y	Y
Country?	N	N	Y	Y
Adj. Rsq	0.7643	0.7795	0.9079	0.9335
Turning point lnGDPpc	10.581	10.362	10.282	9.116
GDPpc ($2,000)	$39,395	$31,644	$29,193	$ 9,102

Regression of country effects from regression B-3 on lnGDPpc2000
   0.0759   −0.0006* lnGDPpc2000   Adj. Rsq 0.0004
   (3.0)   (0.2)

Regression of year effects from regression B-3 on "Year" and "Year squared"
   0.315   −0.00677* "Year" + 0.0000292* "Year"sq   Adj Rsq 0.9375
   (4.9)   (4.3)   (3.1)

SOURCE: Timmer and Akkus 2008, technical annex.
NOTES: a = t– statistics are in parentheses. "Year" = actual year minus 1900. The explanatory variables are logarithm of GDP per capita (lnGDPpc, where GDP per capita is measured in "real" U.S. dollars deflated to the year 2000 and converted at market exchange rates); lnGDPpc squared; and the agricultural to nonagricultural terms of trade (AgToT). The variable to be explained is the share of agricultural employment in total employment (AgEMPshr).

between the agricultural and nonagricultural sectors seen so regularly during the structural transformation.[11]

The share of agriculture in GDP follows a pattern similar to that of employment, but the statistical results are always more significant, and the coefficients become larger rather than smaller as additional statistical controls (separate coefficients for individual years and countries) are added (see the "B" regressions in table 2-2). The decline in the share of GDP for agriculture is much more regular and powerful than the decline in employment share, thus setting up the obvious potential for a mismatch between the two trends. Indeed, the "turning point" for the share of agriculture in a country's economy (that is, when it reaches its statistically estimated minimum level) is always well-defined. But recall that the turning point for the share of employment in agriculture was not well-defined (only the linear term remained significant). It is no wonder that countries seek mechanisms other than economic growth to equilibrate the employment and GDP shares for agriculture.[12]

Although it mostly controls for short-run price movements, the terms-of–trade variable (AgToT) is interesting on its own. Figure 2-1 shows that AgToT exhibits a statistically significant negative trend over time (although the rate of decline is decidedly slower for Asian than for non-Asian countries, a finding discussed in detail below). The variance in the AgToT variable can be decomposed into two sources: that common to all countries from year to year, and the remainder unique to each country and year. A statistical analysis of AgToT itself shows that the "global" market forces at work on domestic economies account for just 20 percent of the variance in the overall AgToT variable. But of this variance explained by global price movements, most (about four-fifths) is accounted for by indices of world food prices, world nonfood agricultural prices, and energy prices.[13]

This finding emphasizes that world markets are a key determinant of the domestic terms of trade between agriculture and nonagriculture for most countries, but most of the variance is due to specific domestic economic and policy factors. Understanding how domestic policy influences the terms of trade between the two sectors is one

FIGURE 2-1
AGRICULTURAL TERMS OF TRADE FOR ASIA AND NON-ASIA
SEPARATELY (2000 = 100)

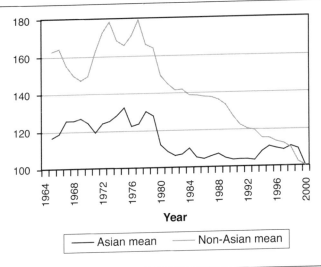

SOURCE: Timmer and Akkus 2008.

essential element in understanding the political economy of the structural transformation, and is discussed below.

Most empirical analysis of the structural transformation has
focused on two variables: agriculture's share in employment and its
share in GDP. The "gap" between the two has often been recognized,
yet it has received little systematic analysis.[14] The present study, by
contrast, takes that gap to be highly meaningful. In the following
pages we focus analysis on that gap—defined for purposes here as the
difference between the share of agriculture in GDP and its share in
employment. This definition consciously causes the gap variable to
be negative in sign for virtually all observations—a visual advantage
in figure 1-1, which shows the gap approaching zero from below.

One advantage of using the difference in shares rather than their
relative values is that the gap variable then translates easily into a
"sectoral Gini coefficient" that indicates the inequality of incomes

(labor productivity) between the two sectors.[15] The negative of the gap variable is equal to the Gini coefficient for agricultural GDP per worker compared with nonagricultural GDP per worker. This "sectoral Gini coefficient" accounts for 20–30 percent of the variation in the overall Gini coefficient for this sample of countries. The rural–urban income gap is a substantial component of a country's overall income inequality and can change rapidly. In China and India, for example, the increase in this gap since the early 1990s has generated strong political pressures.

A worrisome aspect of the rural–urban income gap is that it actually tends to get larger during the early stages of economic growth. The turning point in the relationship for AgGAPshr only occurs at per-capita levels of GDP above $9,000 in regression C-3 in table 2-3 (where the terms-of-trade variable is not included). By way of comparison, per-capita GDP in 2000 was $5,940 in Mexico, $6,185 in Uruguay, $7,700 in Argentina, $10,300 in Greece, and $10,940 in South Korea. The fact that labor productivity in the nonagricultural sector actually increases more rapidly than in the agricultural sector until this turning point is reached, thus exacerbating rural–urban income differences, has much to do with the political difficulties poor countries today will face during a rapid structural transformation.[16]

It is highly revealing that the turning point should come at a lower per-capita income level when the terms-of-trade variable is included in the statistical analysis. Individual countries use agricultural price policy to influence their domestic terms of trade, and this policy instrument helps the growth process to integrate agricultural labor into the rest of the economy, at least in terms of relative productivity.[17] On the other hand, political efforts to influence the domestic terms of trade often run into powerful counterpressures from global commodity markets, and thus require large subsidies or trade barriers to make them effective.

Exogenous forces that are also at work help close the gap in labor productivity, as indicated by the results for the year and country coefficients in the employment and GDP regressions discussed above. The year effects show that closing the gap is getting harder over time,

TABLE 2-3

REGRESSIONS THAT EXPLAIN CHANGES IN THE DIFFERENCE IN THE SHARE OF AGRICULTURE IN GDP AND IN THE LABOR FORCE (THE "GAP") DURING THE STRUCTURAL TRANSFORMATION, 1965–2000

Regression number[a]	Dependent variable: AgGDP share minus AgEMP share equals "AgGAPshr"			
	C-1	C-2	C-3	C-4
Constant	−0.812 (15.1)	−0.907 (16.4)	1.0224 (10.3)	1.318 (15.2)
lnGDPpc	0.0637 (4.3)	0.0771 (5.3)	−0.316 (12.4)	−0.4316 (18.5)
(lnGDPpc)sq.	0.00161 (1.7)	0.000665 (0.7)	0.0173 (9.9)	0.02530 (15.4)
Terms of trade				0.0008327 (29.1)
Year?	N	Y	Y	Y
Country?	N	N	Y	Y
Adj. Rsq	0.5817	0.5944	0.8718	0.9166
Turning point lnGDPpc	—	—	9.133	8.530
GDPpc ($2,000)	—	—	$9,255	$5,063

Regression of country effects from regression C-3 on lnGDPpc2000

−1.033   + 0.1331* lnGDPpc2000   Adj. Rsq 0.8260
(20.2)   (20.0)

Regression of year effects from Regression C-3 on "Year" and "Year squared"
−0.6288 + 0.0136* "Year" − 0.0000584* "Year"sq   Adj Rsq 0.9573
 (5.9)   (5.2)   (5.9)

SOURCE: Timmer and Akkus 2008, technical annex.
NOTES: a = $t-$ statistics are in parentheses. "Year" = actual year minus 1900. The explanatory variables are logarithm of GDP per capita (lnGDPpc, where GDP per capita is measured in "real" U.S. dollars deflated to the year 2000 and converted at market exchange rates); lnGDPpc squared; and the agricultural to nonagricultural terms of trade (AgToT). The variable to be explained is the share of agricultural employment in total employment (AgEMPshr).

and the country effects indicate that richer countries take measures to close it above and beyond the impact from the economic growth process itself. Again, only political mechanisms can explain the use of these measures, although they are closely linked to the wealth of a country and its ability both to finance the budget subsidies and to absorb the subsequent economic distortions that arise.

Changes over Time

One overarching question about the structural transformation is whether it has been a uniform process over time, or whether the very nature of economic growth, and its capacity for integrating "surplus" agricultural workers into the nonagricultural sector, has been changing over the course of history. There are two ways to address the issue. The first is to examine the short-run record of growth using the current sample of countries, with data from 1965 to 2000. That is the task of this section. The second, pursued in the following section, is to examine the long-run record of the early developers to see how their patterns of structural transformation might differ from the modern record.

The Short Run. There are a number of ways to slice the modern record (the 1965–2000 period) of structural transformation into smaller segments. Our goal is to see if any systematic patterns occur over time in either turning points or slopes—and the answer to both is yes. The clearest pattern occurs for the turning points in the gap relationship when the regression includes the terms-of-trade variable. These turning points are as follows:

- 1965–74: $1,109
- 1975–84: $6,379
- 1985–94: $7,880
- 1995–2000: $15,484

Unmistakably, the turning point for the gap in labor productivity between the agricultural and nonagricultural sectors has been steadily rising since the mid-1960s. That is to say, the global economic growth process in our own era has become progressively less successful at integrating low-productivity agricultural labor into the rest of the economy. Complaints that the agricultural economies of poor countries are not well integrated into the growth of the rest of their economies are justified. The reasons for this still need to be understood, but the facts that require explanation are clear enough.

It is possible, of course, that these calculated results stem from a serendipitous choice of time periods rather than from some deep change in the structural transformation itself. But breaking the data into just three time periods instead of four presents an even more striking pattern:[18]

- 1965–79: $1,043

- 1980–90: $19,300

- 1991–2000: $223,044

Such results are strongly suggestive of a failure of modern economic growth processes to integrate the agricultural sectors of poor countries into the rest of their economies, despite relatively successful aggregate growth records.[19]

Perhaps the most striking evidence that the turning point is becoming harder to reach is presented in figure 2-2 (page 25), which shows a nine-year moving average of the calculated turning points for each subsample, starting with 1965–73 and ending with 1992–2000. Although there are ups and downs that seem to be associated with cycles in the global economy, the broad upward movement in this trend is striking. Indeed, by the later years in the sample, even rich countries are no longer guaranteed a place on the converging side of the gap relationship.

A widening sectoral income gap—as differences in labor productivity between urban and rural areas become larger—spells political trouble. Rural households that feel left out of the growth process can vote governments out of office (as in India) or stage protests that threaten civil order and central control (as in China). It is no wonder that policymakers feel compelled to address the problem, and the most visible way is to provide more income to agricultural producers. The long-run way to do this is to raise their labor productivity and encourage agricultural labor to migrate to urban jobs, but the short-run approach—inevitable in most political environments—is to use trade policy to affect domestic agricultural prices.[20] In low-income economies, agricultural protection is a child of growing income inequality between the sectors during the structural transformation. The empirical relationship is demonstrated and analyzed below.

Long-Run Patterns, 1820–1965. Concerns about the distributional impact of globalization are not new. The world economy experienced an earlier round of globalization between 1870 and World War I, and there may be lessons from the currently developed countries that participated in that process. Their economies were experiencing rapid economic growth (by the standards of the time) and facing challenges from the growing integration of labor and capital markets across countries.[21] Thanks to recent work by economic historians, it is possible to examine the nature of these challenges empirically. The results are striking.

First, the patterns from the early developers seem remarkably similar to those for the full sample of countries from 1965 to 2000. Although the small sample size (nine countries with just four observations for all but the United Kingdom) means the coefficients are measured with considerable error, they are still significant by most standards, with the same pattern of signs and magnitudes as for the full sample of contemporary economies.[22]

Second, the tendency for the gap-share variable to widen in the early stages of development does not seem to be a feature just of late-developing countries. To the contrary, the pattern seems equally strong in the early developers. The turning point is in the range of $1,000, depending on exact specifications, and all of the sample countries reached the turning point early in their development. The United Kingdom passed its turning point before 1800, the continental European countries reached it by the mid-1900s, and Japan followed early in the twentieth century. These growth patterns suggest

FIGURE 2-2

NINE-YEAR MOVING AVERAGE OF THE PER-CAPITA GDP LEVEL
FOR THE "TURNING POINT" VS. ACTUAL PER-CAPITA GDP
TRAJECTORIES OF KENYA, THAILAND, MEXICO, AND FRANCE

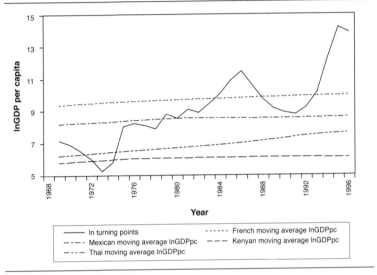

SOURCE: Timmer and Akkus 2008.

that the early experiences for these advanced countries were much
more similar to the international growth patterns of the 1960s and
1970s than to those of the past several decades.

Indeed, virtually the entire growth experience of modern
developed countries has been spent on the convergent path of sectoral labor productivity. This is in sharp contrast to currently developing countries, which are mostly at income levels per capita where
sectoral labor productivity is diverging.

Divergent Paths

There are two ways to think about individual country experiences in
the context of the regular patterns of the structural transformation.
First, all countries might be "unique," so that only the aggregate of

countries would actually display a pattern of transformation over time or across incomes. In this case, the structural transformation would be a long-run phenomenon (over fifty to a hundred years), but not very evident in the short run (during intervals of, say, just five to ten years). Second, most countries might follow some regular pattern over time, with just a handful of "outliers" that deviate significantly from that pattern. In that case, the structural transformation would have both short-run and long-run implications for most countries.

Country Effects. With respect to the basic empirics of the structural transformation, both the *level* and the *slope* of a country's agricultural patterns with respect to per-capita income can vary substantially from the sample-wide patterns. Country effects, which measure the level of a country's position relative to the overall relationship, are fairly large in the employment-share regression. Adding the country effects to regression A-3 in table 2-1, for example, increases the variance explained by eleven percentage points (the adjusted R-squared increases from 0.88 to 0.99). Only six of the eighty-five country effects are *not* statistically significant,[23] and, overall, the country effects are closely related to per-capita GDP. The lnGDPpc variable alone explains 85 percent of the variance in the individual country coefficients. Relatively little additional country variance remains to be explained in the employment-share relationship, and, clearly, the per-capita income effects are utterly dominant.

The country effects are also fairly large in the GDP-share regression.[24] As shown in table 2-2, the R-squared increases from 0.78 in regression B-2 to 0.91 in regression B-3. Only ten of the eighty-five country-effect coefficients lack statistical significance, although the relative size and significance of the coefficients are much smaller for the GDP regressions than for the employment regressions. This statistical pattern reflects the greater degrees of freedom in the political arena to affect labor markets than the share of any sector in the economy.

It is worth noting, however, that the country coefficients in the GDP relationship *are not related at all to per-capita GDP*. Why not, when there is such a strong relationship for the AgEmpshr country effects? This is a major puzzle, and explaining the actual determinants of these country coefficients remains a crucial research task. Likely candidates for the causes include movement in the agricultural to nonagricultural terms of trade, movement in the external terms of trade, openness to foreign trade, composition of exports, and oil importing/exporting status. It is also possible that institutional changes will prove significant, although these are slow to change even over the thirty-five-year horizon represented in our dataset, and thus difficult to measure empirically.

The Contrast between Asia and the Rest of the World. In explaining the gap share, a comparison of the Asian experience with that of all other countries is quite revealing. At first glance, the thirteen Asian countries included in our sample seem to have a pattern of structural transformation between 1965 and 2000 more or less similar to the seventy-three non-Asian countries (see figures 2-3a and 2-3b, page 29). Since the Asian sample includes some of the fastest growing countries during that time period (Japan, Korea, Malaysia, Thailand, and Indonesia), the visual evidence reassures us that there is, in fact, a common, long-run pattern of structural transformation. Statistical analysis, however, reveals significant differences in the patterns.[25] In particular, Asian countries have a very different pattern of agricultural employment change from non-Asian countries with respect to per-capita incomes.

For Asian countries, the linear term in lnGDPpc is positive, and the quadratic term is negative—just the opposite of the non-Asian sample, signaling that Asian economies tend to employ disproportionately more farm workers in the early stages of development. More critically, the coefficient on the agricultural terms of trade is *positive* and statistically significant for the Asian sample, whereas it is *negative* and statistically significant for the non-Asian sample. In this, the Asian pattern contrasts with the overall sample as well.

The impact is fairly clear—Asian countries were able to use the agricultural terms of trade as a policy instrument for keeping labor employed in agriculture, a pattern not seen in the rest of the countries in the sample. Average economic growth in the Asian sample was faster than in the rest of the countries, and the rapid decline in the share of GDP from agriculture reflects this rapid growth. Although the pattern of signs in the AgGDPshr regressions is the same for both samples, the coefficient on the agricultural terms of trade is three times larger in the Asian than the non-Asian sample, reflecting the heavier reliance on this policy tool to mitigate the consequences of rapid growth: a widening gap in labor productivity between the agricultural and nonagricultural sectors.

The implication is that Asian countries provided more price incentives to their agricultural sectors over this time period as a way to prevent the movement of labor out of agriculture from being "too fast." Certainly, the pattern of movements in the agricultural terms of trade for the two sets of countries is strikingly different, with the Asian countries seeing a long-run decline at half the pace of the non-Asian countries (already seen in figure 2-1). The political economy of these choices is explored below, where the agricultural terms of trade are split into two components, one dependent on world prices for agricultural commodities and energy, the second a residual reflecting domestic factors in the formation of the agricultural terms of trade.

The net effect of these forces on the gap between labor productivity in the two sectors is that the turning point in the gap relationship (after which labor productivity in agriculture begins to converge with labor productivity in nonagriculture) is sharply lower in the Asian sample. The turning point for the Asian countries is just $1,600, whereas it is over $11,000 for the non-Asian countries— over six times higher. This difference underscores two distinctive features of the Asian economies: their more rapid growth and the greater role of agricultural productivity in that growth.[26]

The reasons for these differences have been the source of considerable debate. An explanation that resonates with the empirical results reported here is that Asian countries were more concerned about providing "macro" food security in urban markets and "micro" food security to rural households because of large and dense populations farming on very limited agricultural resources. Political stability, and with it the foundation for modern economic growth, grew out of an approach to the provision of food security that connected

FIGURE 2-3a

THE STRUCTURAL TRANSFORMATION FOR THIRTEEN ASIAN COUNTRIES

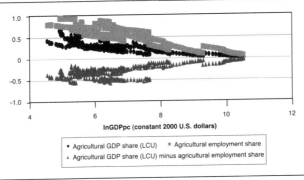

SOURCE: Timmer and Akkus 2008.

NOTES: Figure 2-3a shows the declining share of agriculture in employment (squares), in economic output (circles), and the gap between these two shares (triangles), as per-capita incomes increase (see figure 1-1 for the same patterns for all countries combined). The thirteen Asian countries represented are Bangladesh, China, India, Indonesia, Japan, Korea, Malaysia, Nepal, Pakistan, Papua New Guinea, Philippines, Sri Lanka, and Thailand.

FIGURE 2-3b

THE STRUCTURAL TRANSFORMATION FOR SEVENTY-THREE NON-ASIAN COUNTRIES

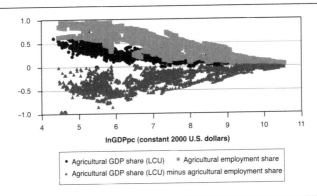

SOURCE: Timmer and Akkus 2008.

NOTE: Figure 2-3b shows the declining share of agriculture in employment (squares), in economic output (circles), and the gap between these two shares (triangles), as per-capita incomes increase (see figure 1-1 for the same patterns for all countries combined).

poor households to improved opportunities.[27] These arguments are detailed in the second half of the monograph.

Policy Responses

The distinct patterns of structural transformation from Asia suggest that country-specific policies have the potential to alter not just the tempo of economic growth (a fact long and widely recognized), but also the structural character of that growth. That dual potential has sparked a policy debate, especially with respect to the role of agriculture, over the determinants of "pro-poor growth," a somewhat infelicitous term that is increasingly being replaced by the equally vague "inclusive" growth.[28] Whatever the term, connecting the poor to rapid economic growth is a desirable policy objective.

This is no place to review the entire debate, but it is possible to examine the impact on the structural transformation of policy choices in one especially relevant area: agricultural prices. The key role of the agricultural terms of trade in conditioning the path of structural change has already been discussed—but those were the *actual* terms of trade reflected in an economy, not necessarily the terms of trade desired by policymakers. It is possible to go a step further to examine those policy desires, what drives them, and their impact.

Understanding the Formation of the Agricultural Terms of Trade. Most agricultural price policies are implemented through either trade interventions or subsidies. Our goal here is *not* to understand the design, or implementation, of actual agricultural trade policies; for that, the classic Krueger, Schiff, and Valdes study of agricultural price distortions, and the ongoing update of that work by Kym Anderson and his colleagues, can provide much valuable information.[29] Here, instead, we examine how agricultural price policy evolves over the long-run course of structural transformation, using GDP deflators from national income accounts as the source of data on sectoral price changes.

In this analysis, the agricultural to nonagricultural terms of trade

(AgToT—that is, the ratio between the GDP deflator for agricultural value added in national income accounts and the GDP deflator for value added in the rest of the economy) is our starting point for constructing a proxy for desired agricultural trade policy. With this variable, we can focus exclusively on the *price effects* of agricultural trade policy; quantity effects are treated elsewhere.[30] The *mechanics* of the implementation of trade policy are largely ignored.

Of course, agricultural price *policies* are only one of the many variables that influence the actual domestic AgToT. Many of the influencing variables are beyond the direct influence of policymakers, such as the real exchange rate, international commodity prices, and the changing structure of the economy during economic development.[31] Agricultural trade policies are, by design, things that policymakers can change according to their priorities. When we control for these exogenous factors influencing agricultural prices over the process of development, the changing level and impact of agricultural price policies can be identified in the statistical record.

How are agricultural prices set? We argue that there is a link between sectoral income distribution and policy response, in the form of changes in the domestic input to the agricultural terms of trade. Political pressures caused by a rising gap between incomes in the agricultural and nonagricultural sectors lead policymakers to improve incentives for agricultural producers.

Two steps are required to test the significance of this link empirically. First, to create a price variable that reflects *intentions* of policymakers, the AgToT series for each country needs to be "purged" of impact from prices in world markets over which individual countries have little or no control. As already noted, common price movements in world markets (the year coefficients in the overall AgToT regression) explain just 20 percent of total variance in the AgToT variable. This assumes, however, that all countries have the same relationship with world markets and prices. Thus, the first step is to relax that assumption and generate a new agricultural terms-of-trade series that is net of world prices—a variable we term the "domestic policy agricultural terms of trade."[32]

The second step is to explain the year-to-year fluctuations in this new domestic price policy variable. Our hypothesis is that widening sectoral income inequality is a major driver of domestic farm price policy, and this is tested by making the domestic policy agricultural terms of trade a function of AgGAPshr (equal to the negative of the sectoral Gini coefficient).[33]

The annual average terms-of-trade variable is significantly related to three key price series from world markets—a food price index, an index of agricultural nonfood raw materials, and real crude oil prices—with a +, −, − pattern to the signs. Varying economic structures and levels of development, however, would suggest that not all countries will follow this pattern. Since the interest here is in country-specific policy initiatives to cope with the pressures of changing income distribution during the structural transformation, it is necessary to let each country have its own response to this set of world prices.

The results are, predictably, complex and heterogeneous.[34] Even so: Instead of just 20 percent of the variance in domestic AgToT being explained by common world prices,[35] the regressions, when run separately, explain about three times as much of the formation of domestic agricultural prices relative to nonagricultural prices.

With these statistical results in hand, it is possible to generate a *predicted* value of each country's agricultural terms of trade for each year based on prices in world markets. From this new series a variable reflecting just the influence of domestic policy on the terms of trade is created, as the difference between the predicted and actual terms-of-trade value. It is centered on 100 and has no distinguishable time trend, since this was already captured by the strong time trends in all three world-price series.

It has taken several steps, both logically and statistically, to reach this stage. But the results are worth the effort. In its simplest specification, the question is whether domestic policymakers are influenced by changing sectoral income distribution during the structural transformation, and whether this influence can be seen in the formation of the "domestic policy" agricultural terms of trade.

The most persuasive result is the simplest. At mean values, the (highly significant) elasticity of domestic agricultural terms of trade with respect to the gap between labor productivity in the agricultural sector as compared to the nonagricultural sector is about 0.25. In statistical terms, *the full fixed-effects model shows a highly significant response of domestic policymakers to changes in the sectoral distribution of income, after controlling for year and country effects.*

The overall explanatory power of this simple regression is relatively small (the adjusted R-squared is only 0.17), but, as was noted, many other considerations are likely to go into the formation of domestic price policy, including political structure, that are not included here. In addition, substantial "noise" in this variable is to be expected given the way in which it was constructed, as a residual from the regression of year- and country-specific agricultural terms of trade on world prices for food, agricultural nonfood raw materials, and oil.

The year and country coefficients in this regression exhibit statistically significant patterns with respect to time (for the year coefficients) and real per-capita incomes in 2000 (for the country coefficients). In both cases, the relationship is positive.[36] Thus, the variable for domestic policy agricultural terms of trade is increasing over time, independently of what is happening to the sectoral distribution of income. But figure 2-2 has also shown that the turning point in the GAP relationship with respect to real per-capita incomes is rising rapidly—and, thus, sectoral income distribution is widening—*so domestic policy formation is stimulated by both factors.*

In addition, richer countries do more to protect their agricultural sectors than poorer countries (in the form of higher values of the domestic policy agricultural terms of trade), even after controlling for the time effect and the pressures from the sectoral Gini itself. This overall pattern has been well known for some time;[37] but from this more disaggregated perspective, agricultural protection can be seen to be a modest economic "necessity," as the income elasticity implied in the statistical results is positive but less than 1. For the countries in this sample, this income elasticity is about 0.055. Although the income elasticity for this "pure" form of agricultural protection is small, it is highly significant in economic terms. In a world where real income differentials between rich and poor countries span a twentyfold scale, a "mere" 0.055 elasticity has some very dramatic implications for differential price support—more than a tripling.

How the Asian Experience Differs in Agricultural Price Policy. Somewhat ironically, the response of Asian countries to the growing gap in labor productivity between the agricultural and nonagricultural sectors is less sensitive than in non-Asian countries. The irony, of course, is that Asian countries have used agricultural price policy very aggressively to protect their farmers, especially in the rapidly growing countries of East Asia.[38] Their agricultural terms of trade declined at only half the rate as for non-Asian countries, despite being subject to the same global market forces (see figure 2-1). But the very speed of the Asian transformation, and the greater concentration on (and success in) raising the productivity of small farmers, means that the actual coefficient of policy response to the AgGAPshr variable (the sectoral Gini) is smaller than in the non-Asian countries.

Recall that the turning point for the AgGAPshr regression for Asian countries was just $1,663, compared with a turning point of $11,329 for non-Asian countries.[39] Asian countries devoted greater policy attention to agriculture across the board, and had the advantage of more equal landholdings than in most other countries. As a result, Asian countries were able to generate a far more rapid and inclusive pattern of economic growth (with several exceptions, the Philippines being perhaps the most obvious). The sheer pace of Asian growth created great political pressures to assist agriculture during the transformation process, but, in comparative terms, non-Asian countries had to resort to interventions in price policies more heavily in response to widening income distribution from their less rapidly growing economies. That is, the economies of Asian countries responded more flexibly to movements in their agricultural terms of trade, which somewhat paradoxically meant that Asian policymakers could respond somewhat less aggressively to a growing gap in sectoral incomes. They kept the gap from growing too large in the first place.

This effect can be seen even more clearly when both components of the agricultural terms of trade are included separately in the standard structural transformation regressions, for Asia and non-Asia (see

TABLE 2-4

IMPACTS OF THE PREDICTED AGRICULTURAL TERMS OF
TRADE FOR ASIA AND NON-ASIA

Asia			
	Impact of the specified agricultural terms of trade on . . .		
	AgEMPshr	AgGDPshr	AgGAPshr
Predicted AgToT (t)	0.000590 (7.1)	0.001926 (30.2)	0.001336
Domestic policy AgToT (t)	−0.000138 (1.2)	−0.001563 (17.7)	−0.001425
Adj R sq	0.9854	0.9772	

Non-Asia			
	Impact of the specified agricultural terms of trade on . . .		
	AgEMPshr	AgGDPshr	AgGAPshr
Predicted AgToT (t)	−0.000163 (7.4)	0.000604 (21.9)	0.000767
Domestic policy AgToT (t)	0.0000521 (1.8)	−0.000663 (18.7)	−0.000715
Adj R sq	0.9886	0.9341	

SOURCE: Timmer and Akkus 2008, technical annex.
NOTES: All regressions also include lnGDPpc and (lnGPDpc)squared, as well as year and country fixed effects. The AgGAPshr coefficient is calculated as the difference between the AgGDPshr
and AgEMPshr coefficients. The coefficients show the separate impacts of the predicted agricultural terms of trade based on world prices, and the residual domestic agricultural terms of
trade that reflect policy preferences, for Asia and non-Asia separately.

table 2-4).[40] The results are not surprising in view of what has
already been reported, but they are powerful nonetheless. In Asia,
the predicted AgToT (that is, the world price component) has a
positive and significant impact on *both* the share of agriculture in
employment and its share in GDP. Because AgGAPshr is defined in

such a way that it is negative for nearly all observations, the net impact of higher world agricultural and energy prices in Asian countries (through their impact on the overall domestic agricultural terms of trade) is to *reduce* the level of income inequality. In sharp contrast, the impact of domestic policy AgToT is negative, although the coefficient on AgEMPshr is not significant. Reverse causation seems to be the only plausible explanation for such an impact, with widening sectoral income distribution actually causing domestic agricultural policy to respond with greater price incentives.

The broader role of agriculture revealed in these patterns extends well beyond agricultural price policy, and it clearly is powerful enough to influence the basic patterns of the structural transformation. It is important, then, to understand what role agriculture actually plays on the way to its virtual disappearance as a share of the economy. It turns out that a "world without agriculture" cannot happen without first investing in the sector in financial and policy terms. What needs to be done is the subject of the following chapters.

3

The Paradoxical Role of Agriculture in the Structural Transformation

Interest in agriculture declined in the 1980s, and that brought a concomitant decline in efforts to understand the continuing role of the sector in both economic growth and poverty reduction.[1] That decline slowed gradually in the late 1990s, and a new resurgence of interest has been apparent since food prices started rising in the mid-2000s. Part of the resurgence is just fashionable—the United Nations' Millennium Development Goals, with their focus on poverty, have captured donor attention, and most of the very poor still live in rural areas. But part comes with a new realization that agriculture is the "greenest" of industries and the major pathway for putting solar energy to effective economic use. (This fact drives the current interest in biofuels.)

The past decade has brought a quiet revolution in the understanding of determinants of poverty and the mechanisms for reducing it in a sustainable fashion. Partly, it is a simple recognition that economic growth is the main vehicle for reducing poverty—provided the distribution of income does not widen too sharply. In many modern settings, growth in the agricultural sector has been an important ingredient in the formula that connects economic growth to the poor, and the fact that most of the poor and hungry are in rural areas has renewed attention to stimulating rural economic growth.[2] Agriculture will play a key role in this effort.

Furthermore, after decades of almost steady decline, international food prices have been rising since 2002. Increased demand for agricultural commodities (food staples such as cereals and vegetable oils), as well as for industrial raw materials to feed biofuel processing plants, has pushed up prices across the board. This increased demand comes partly from rapid economic growth in a few of the large low-income countries, notably China and India, and partly from prolonged weakness in the U.S. dollar.[3] However, the emergence of high energy prices since 2005 and a growing international consensus that immediate steps must be taken to slow the pace of climate change have also stimulated an investment boom in biofuels, and hence interest in agricultural productivity.

While the renewed interest in agricultural growth is welcome (if rather overdue), it is also well to note that the sources of such growth are likely to be sharply different in the next several decades from those witnessed in the immediate past. There will be less reliance on area expansion and new irrigation investments, and more reliance on modern biology (to develop greater yield potential), as well as improved management techniques that will be highly site-specific. Climate change will almost certainly be a significant challenge to plant breeders and farmers alike.[4] And the pace of supply response to the new demand environment is highly uncertain as of 2008, although historical evidence is reasonably reassuring with regard to the medium to long run.[5]

The Role of Agriculture in Economic Development

The role of agriculture in economic development is complicated and controversial, despite a long historical literature examining the topic.[6] Part of the controversy stems from the structural transformation itself, which is a general equilibrium process not easily understood from within the agricultural sector.[7] Over long historical periods, agriculture's role seems to evolve through four basic stages (see figure 3-1 on page 41):

- The early "Mosher" environment, when "getting agriculture moving" is the main policy objective.[8]

- The "Johnston-Mellor" environment, when agriculture contributes to economic growth through a variety of linkages.[9]

- The "T. W. Schultz-V. Ruttan" environment, when rising

agricultural incomes still fall behind those in a rapidly growing nonagricultural economy, inducing serious political tensions.[10]

- The "D. Gale Johnson" environment, when labor and financial markets fully integrate the agricultural economy into the rest of the economy.[11]

These environments, or stages, were first proposed by Timmer in 1988 and are further developed in the context of more recent experience with the World Bank's treatment of the role of agriculture in reducing poverty.[12] Efforts to "skip" the early stages and jump directly to a modern industrial economy have generally courted disaster.

Controversy over the role of agriculture in economic development also stems from the heterogeneity of agricultural endowments and the vastly different cropping systems seen in Latin America, Africa, and Asia (not to mention the diversity within these regions). It is unrealistic to expect much of a common role in such diverse settings. When coupled with the enormous differences in stages of development around the world, and hence the vastly different roles that agriculture plays in economies at different levels of economic maturity, it is easy to understand why there is so little consensus in academia or the donor community.[13]

The literature does seem to hold widespread agreement on the basic linkages connecting agriculture and overall economic growth, which were first articulated to a general economics audience by Lewis, Johnston and Mellor, and Johnston and Kilby.[14] At a conceptual level, these linkages have long been part of the core of modern development theory and practice,[15] and establishing the empirical value of these linkages in different settings has been a cottage industry since the early 1970s.[16]

Virtually all of the studies have concluded that the "agriculture multiplier" is significantly greater than 1, especially in relatively closed, "nontradable" economies of the sort found in rural Africa, where it is often between 2 and 3. But even in the more open economies of Asia, where rice is more tradable than most African staple foods and local prices more easily reflect border prices, the agriculture multiplier is close to 2 in the early stages of agricultural modernization when productivity gains are fastest. Because economic growth usually has a direct impact on poverty, any contribution agriculture makes to speeding overall economic growth through these large multipliers will, in most circumstances, also directly contribute to reducing poverty.[17]

Despite the potential impact of these large multipliers, a combination of market failures and political biases has led to a systematic undervaluation of output from rural economies. Correcting these biases can have economy-wide benefits. The historical bias against the rural sector in developing countries has left them starved for resources and discriminated against by macroeconomic and trade policies.[18] Failures in rural credit and labor markets—some of which can cause "poverty traps"—have provided the analytical context for much of modern neoclassical development economics.[19] But even global commodity markets for many products from developing countries "fail" in the sense that agricultural surpluses from rich countries are dumped there, depressing world market prices below long-run costs of production.

A final set of linkages makes growth originating in the agricultural sector tend to be more "pro-poor" than it would be if the source were the industrial or service sectors.[20] New agricultural technologies that improve farm productivity strengthen this connection. Separate reviews by Thirtle and others and by Majid confirm the strong empirical link between higher agricultural productivity and poverty reduction,[21] as has research conducted for the World Bank's *World Development Report, 2008: Agriculture for Development*.[22]

Direct Contribution to Economic Growth via Lewis Linkages. The "Lewis linkages" between agriculture and economic growth provide the nonagricultural sector with labor and capital freed up by higher productivity in the agricultural sector. These linkages work primarily through factor markets, but there is no suggestion that these markets work perfectly in the dualistic setting analyzed by Lewis.[23] Chenery and Syrquin have argued that a major source of economic growth is the transfer of low-productivity labor from the rural to the urban sector.[24] If labor markets worked perfectly,

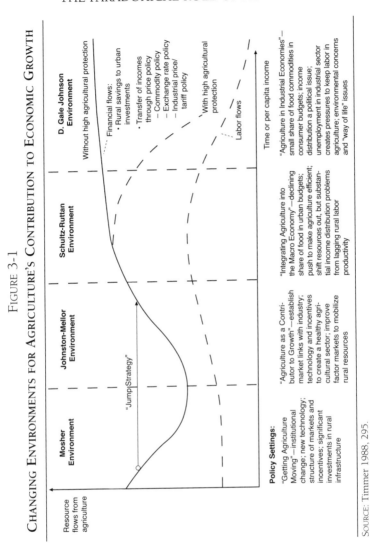

FIGURE 3-1

CHANGING ENVIRONMENTS FOR AGRICULTURE'S CONTRIBUTION TO ECONOMIC GROWTH

SOURCE: Timmer 1988, 295.

there would be few productivity gains from this structural transfer, a point emphasized by Syrquin in more recent work.[25]

Indirect Contributions to Economic Growth via Johnston-Mellor Linkages. The "Johnston-Mellor linkages" allow market-mediated, input–output interactions between the two sectors so that agriculture can contribute to economic development. These linkages are based on the agricultural sector's supplying raw materials to industry, food for industrial workers, markets for industrial output, and exports to earn the foreign exchange needed to import capital goods.[26] Again, for the Johnston-Mellor linkages—as with the Lewis linkages—it is difficult to see any significance for policy or economic growth unless some of the markets that serve these linkages are operating imperfectly (or, as with many risk markets, are missing altogether). That is, resource allocations must be out of equilibrium and face constraints and bottlenecks not immediately reflected in market prices if increases in agricultural output are to stimulate the rest of the economy at a rate that causes the "contribution" from agriculture to be greater than the market value of the output—in other words, the agricultural income multiplier must be greater than 1.[27]

Contributions from Agriculture to Economic Growth That Are Hard to Measure. Writing in the mid-1960s, Mosher was able to assume that "getting agriculture moving" would have a high priority in national plans because of its "obvious" importance in feeding people and providing a spur to industrialization.[28] That assumption has held only in parts of East and Southeast Asia, and has been badly off the mark in much of Africa and Latin America. In the latter regions, a historically prolonged and deep urban bias led to a distorted pattern of investment. Too much public and private capital was invested in urban areas and too little in rural areas. Too much capital was held as liquid and nonproductive investments that rural households used to manage risk. Too little was invested in raising rural productivity.

Such distortions resulted in strikingly different marginal productivities of capital in urban and rural areas. New growth strategies—such as those pursued in Indonesia after 1966, China after 1978, and Vietnam after 1989—altered investment priorities in favor of rural growth and benefited from this disequilibrium in rates of return, at least initially. For example, in Indonesia from the mid-1960s to the mid-1990s, real value added per farm worker increased by nearly half, whereas it had apparently declined from 1900 through the mid-1960s. In China, the increase from 1978 to 1994 was nearly 70 percent, whereas this measure had dropped by 20 percent between 1935 and 1978.[29] A switch in investment strategy and improved rates of return on capital increase factor productivity (and farm income) because efficiency in resource allocation is improved.

One explanation for more rapid and inclusive economic growth as urban bias is reduced is provided by Mellor's model of agricultural growth, rural employment, and poverty reduction, which emphasizes the role of the rural nontradables sector in pulling underemployed workers out of agriculture and into the nonagricultural rural economy. The Mellor model explicitly integrates manufactured export performance (the source of much dynamism in East Asia's economies since the 1960s) and the nontradables sector in the rural economy (which includes a wide array of local agro-processing) to explain subsequent reductions in poverty. This model, drawing on Mellor's earlier work in India[30] and, more recently, in Egypt,[31] explains why countries with substantial agricultural sectors that experienced rapid growth from labor-intensive manufactured exports had such good records of overall economic growth and poverty reduction.

An additional set of linkages focuses on more nebulous and hard-to-measure connections between growth in agricultural productivity and growth in the rest of the economy. These linkages grow explicitly out of market failures, and, if they are quantitatively important, government interventions are required for the growth process to proceed as rapidly as possible. The contribution of agriculture to productivity growth in the nonagricultural economy stems from several sources: greater efficiency in decision-making as rural enterprises claim a larger share of output, and higher productivity of industrial capital as urban bias is reduced; higher productivity of labor as nutritional standards are improved; and a link between agricultural profitability (as distinct from agricultural *productivity*) and household investments in rural human capital, which raises labor productivity as well as facilitates rural–urban migration.

Several of these mechanisms stand out as potentially important (and potentially measurable) because they capitalize on the efficiency of decision-making in rural households, the low opportunity cost of their labor resources, the opportunity for farm investment without the need for financial intermediaries, and the potential to earn high rates of return on public investments that correct for urban bias. Alone, each of these factors should cause an increase in the efficiency of resource allocation as public investments and favorable policy stimulate growth in the agricultural sector. In combination, these mechanisms should translate faster agricultural growth into measurably faster economic growth in aggregate, after controlling for the direct contribution of the agricultural sector to growth in GDP itself.[32]

One of the most visible determinants of poverty is hunger and malnutrition. The development profession continues to argue over causation—whether hunger causes poverty or vice versa—but hunger as a *measure* of poverty is widely established. Most poverty lines have an explicit or implicit food component. The evidence for nutritional poverty traps, where workers are too malnourished to work hard enough to feed themselves and their families, has strong historical roots.[33] But simple energy shortages cannot account for very much of the chronic poverty observed over the past several decades, because the cost of raw calories, in the form of staple foods, has fallen sharply relative to wages for unskilled labor.[34] If *inadequate food intake* is the primary cause of poverty, the solution would be in sight (and food aid could be an important part of the answer). If, however, *poverty* is the main cause of inadequate food intake, hunger will be much harder to end. In most countries, the domestic agricultural sector is likely to play a key role in ending hunger (and a too-ready availability of food aid might actually be part of the problem).

Linking Agriculture to Poverty Reduction

In current strategies used by countries and donor agencies to cope with poverty, the role of agriculture has been limited, largely because of a failure to recognize the importance of direct links among agricultural development, food availability, caloric intake by the poor, and poverty reduction. In part, poverty reduction is definitional because the poverty line is often measured in caloric terms. But raising the caloric intake of the poor has a positive effect on their well-being, work productivity, and investment in human capital. Empirical evidence provided by Paul Schultz and by Fogel illustrates this importance,[35] but a more general case can also be made.

The case builds on three empirical relationships: between agricultural growth and poverty alleviation; between increases in domestic food production and improvements in nutrient intake; and between agricultural productivity and productivity growth in the rest of the economy. It has long been established that, for a given level of income per capita, a higher share of GDP originating in agriculture contributes to a more equal distribution of income, and recent empirical work confirms that message.[36] An agriculture-driven growth strategy, if it does not sacrifice aggregate growth, directs a greater share of income to the poor—that is, it is more pro-poor. Such a strategy is the first step in breaking the cycle of poverty.

Next, increases in domestically produced food supplies contribute *directly* to increases in average caloric intake per capita, after controlling for changes in income per capita, income distribution, and food prices.[37] Countries with rapidly increasing food production have much better records of poverty alleviation, perhaps because of changes in the local economics of access to food—changes that are not captured by aggregate statistics on incomes and prices. The most recent confirmation of this relationship is in the 2004 study by Majid, mentioned above. With the $1 per day head-count poverty rate from the International Labor Organization (ILO) dataset as the dependent variable, *both* the log of agricultural output per worker *and* the per-capita food production index have a large and statistically significant impact on reducing poverty (controlling for per-capita income and other standard variables).[38]

Whatever the mechanisms, intensive campaigns to raise domestic food production—through rural investments and rapid technological change—can be expected to have positive spillover effects on nutrient intake among the poor. Raising food productivity is the second step in breaking the cycle of poverty.

The third step is to ensure that these sectoral gains can be sustained without distorting the economy or destroying the environment. These dual goals can be achieved only if factor productivity increases for the entire economy. Eventually, growth in factor productivity must provide a substantial share of total growth in income per capita. When using its resource base efficiently, agriculture has a key role to play at this stage, as well.[39]

Agriculture has been seriously undervalued by both the public and private sectors in those societies in which poverty has remained untouched (or, in some cases, has even deepened). That is, market prices for basic food commodities have reflected both *market* and *government* failures in sending appropriate signals about the full social value of increased output—a value that needs to include the value that society places on poverty reduction and reduced hunger, as well as the incremental value to GDP.[40]

The government failures are reflected largely in pervasive urban bias in domestic policies (although corruption and inefficiency in the design and implementation of rural projects contributes, as well). The market failures are seen in commodity prices that, by not valuing reduced hunger or progress against poverty, often do not send signals with appropriate incentives to decision-makers. Their absence causes several problems, in addition to those noted above.

First, low values for agricultural commodities in the marketplace are reflected in low political commitments. Higher commitments to rural growth are needed to generate a more balanced economy, with less urban bias than has been seen in most developing countries historically.[41] Since the late 1980s, the developing world has seen a notable reduction in the macroeconomic biases against agriculture, such as overvalued currencies, repression of financial systems, and exploitive terms of trade.[42] Further progress might be expected as democracy spreads and empowers the rural population in poor countries (although agricultural policies in most democracies make economists cringe).

The second problem with low valuation of agricultural commodities is that rural labor is also undervalued. This weakens the link between urban and rural labor markets, a link that is often manifested in the form of seasonal migration and remittances. There is no hope of reducing rural poverty without rising real wages for rural workers. Rising wages have a demand and a supply dimension, and migration can affect both in ways that support higher living standards in both parts of the economy. Migration of workers from rural to urban areas raises other issues, of course, but those issues depend fundamentally on whether this migration is driven by the push of rural poverty or the pull of urban jobs.[43]

Either way, the food security dimensions of rural–urban migration are clear. Urban markets become relatively more important in supplying food needs for the population. Whether the country's own rural economy or the world market is the best source of that supply is one of the prime strategic issues facing economic policymakers and trade negotiators.[44] It is no accident that China, through its commitments upon entering the World Trade Organization (WTO), decided to use world markets to provision a significant share of its basic food supply. The intent was to keep food costs low and stable and thus provide a competitive advantage to its labor-intensive industries and producers of high-value agricultural commodities. Beijing sees few long-run income opportunities for small-scale producers of staple grains. At the same time, leaders are troubled by instability in world grain markets and will try to make domestic grain production profitable enough to ensure a substantial degree of self-sufficiency, a difficult balancing act.

From Agricultural to Rural Development

The rural nonfarm sector is usually the bridge between commodity-based agriculture—which is often on a "treadmill" between rising productivity and falling prices[45]—and livelihoods earned in the modern industrial and service sectors in urban centers. Throughout Asia, most rural households earn half or more of their income from nonfarm sources, and often this sector is the "ladder" from underemployment at farm tasks to regular wage employment in the local economy, and from there to jobs in the formal sector.[46]

The two major constraints on expanding the rural nonfarm sector are inadequate demand and lack of access to finance.[47] Historically, the first constraint has been addressed through higher farm incomes and greater agricultural productivity. As to the second, governments have tried a plethora of credit schemes to help rural firms (and farms), few of which have worked.

A certain enthusiasm has grown since the early 1990s for market-based rural finance initiatives that circumvent the problems faced by earlier efforts to provide subsidized credit to small enterprises and farmers so they could adopt modern technologies.[48] By tapping local villagers' knowledge of each other's capacities to repay loans, grassroots microfinance operations have been widely established to provide vehicles for risk management and household savings. Unfortunately, there is little significant evidence that these operations actually contribute to economic growth. Somewhat more surprising, the evidence is thin that such schemes even reduce broad-based poverty in a sustainable fashion.[49]

What does seem to work, but is much more difficult to implement, is a formal system of rural–urban financial intermediation that improves factor mobility. Linking small, rural, local savings to investment opportunities outside the rural economy is arguably an important way to help households maximize returns on their capital, to create incentives to save, and to smooth the flow of resources out of agriculture as part of the structural transformation. Establishing these linkages, however, requires reasonably large financial institutions that are able to establish branch offices in rural areas and tap modern financial instruments in urban areas. Such institutions tend not to spring up from rural roots.

4

Is Agricultural Development More Difficult Now? New Challenges and New Opportunities

The new challenges facing agricultural development are unmistakable, especially in the poorest countries where it is needed most. Globalization has brought new sources of demand, but they come with high safety and environmental standards that are enforced by modern supply chains. And globalization is a two-edged sword, because it also brings new supplies to these countries, competing effectively with local farmers and traditional food marketing chains. All of the early indications from models of climate change are that farmers in sub-Saharan Africa will be adversely affected as temperatures rise and drought becomes even more prevalent than it is now. The new demand for biofuels would seem to be a big bonus for agricultural producers of the raw materials for this industry, but if the net impact is higher food prices facing the poor and greater environmental degradation in the rush to expand production, the bonus might be small, indeed. Finally, the gap is widening between labor productivity in the agricultural and nonagricultural sectors, presenting a major challenge to policymakers seeking to stay on a balanced path during the structural transformation.

Creating a dynamic and efficient agriculture was never easy, but by comparison with the period since the mid-1980s, policymakers in the 1960s and 1970s faced a substantially different, and arguably more advantageous, environment for creating the right public and private investments in rural economies.[1] The differences fall into five basic categories:

49

- "New" and more difficult initial conditions confronting policymakers

- Rising opposition from rich countries, both in the form of protection of their own farmers and concerns over losing their export markets

- A relatively stagnant shelf of available agricultural technologies that can be easily borrowed and widely adopted by farmers

- International aid donors who have been distracted from their core mission by development fads and pressures from "single-issue" interest groups

- A new connection between food and fuel prices that complicates the design of appropriate food policies.

The Department for International Development characterizes the core argument of these issues into two camps: the "smallholder optimists" and the "smallholder pessimists." The debate between them is sharp:

> There is probably less of a consensus now—particularly amongst development agencies—on the best (in terms of impact on poverty and hunger) agricultural development strategy than at any time over the last half-century or longer. . . . This is particularly true of Africa, where an unsuccessful model based on improving performance through technology supported by publicly owned development agencies has been replaced by the equally disappointing response of farmers to the liberalization of markets.[2]

The smallholder pessimists, such as Maxwell,[3] argue that small-scale agriculture is becoming increasingly uncompetitive in the face of the revolution in supply chains and the globalization of food trade. The smallholder optimists, on the other hand, led by Lipton and scholars at the International Food Policy Research Institute (IFPRI), hold that the historic relationships between agriculture and economic growth still hold, especially in Africa, where smallholders are "protected" by high transportation costs and the cultivation of many nontradable food commodities.[4] Naturally, the policy conclusions of the two camps are totally different. Their positions turn fundamentally on the question of whether it is possible to skip the stage of agricultural modernization in the structural transformation (as in the "jump strategy" illustrated in figure 3-1).

"New" Initial Conditions

The initial success of the Green Revolution (which sparked agriculture as the engine of pro-poor economic growth in the 1960s) was in East, Southeast, and South Asia. Seemingly difficult initial conditions— heavy population pressures against available arable land, poorly educated and overwhelmingly rural populations, deep and widespread poverty—turned out to be precisely what made investments in new agricultural technology and rural infrastructure highly profitable. Today's very poor countries in Africa and Central Asia, on the other hand, face low population densities in their low productivity areas; hence, building rural infrastructure to raise productivity in these areas seems prohibitively expensive.

Second, the real prices of agricultural commodities have been very low in historical terms, thus making it difficult to justify investments whose payoff will be increased production of exactly these low-valued commodities. Since 1974, the real price of rice in world markets dropped from over $2,500 per metric ton (in constant 2007 dollars) to $200 per metric ton, reaching its historic low in 2002.[5] After that, rice prices climbed gradually until they roughly doubled by 2007 and then spiraled upward in 2008, doubling yet again. Many other agricultural commodity prices followed a similar trend.[6] Even so, most grain prices remained well below their peaks in the previous world food crisis of 1973–74, and they have declined significantly since their most recent peaks in May 2008. By November, food prices remained above their twenty- to thirty-year trend levels, but worries about the "food crisis" were replaced by worries about the "financial crisis" (which is partly responsible for the sharp drop in commodity prices during the second half of 2008). With average farm size decreasing in most countries due to population growth, finding a technology package and farm-gate price that will increase farm household incomes above the poverty line is substantially harder now than in the mid-1970s.[7]

Third, the easy investments in hospitable environments, especially for irrigation infrastructure, have mostly been made. In the same fashion, high-yielding seed technology for widely uniform planting environments has been developed. What remains are the more distant, more difficult, and less productive agricultural settings that have been bypassed by the mainstream of the Green Revolution. To add to the difficulties, the international community today is more concerned about environmental degradation, whether from expanding cultivated areas into tropical rain forests, upstream and downstream impacts from construction of large dams, or simply the impact on fragile ecosystems of highly intensive cropping systems. These environmental concerns have substantially raised the bar for any large-scale investments in agricultural output—or at least any with donor financing.

In combination, the initial conditions facing the currently poorest countries (and regions)—precisely those bypassed by the first Green Revolution—are far more difficult than those that faced the successful countries in East, Southeast, and South Asia. The obvious question (one without an obvious answer) is whether agricultural development is now simply too expensive, or too controversial, to pursue as the engine of pro-poor growth, even for those countries where the vast majority of the poor are farmers.

Opposition and Higher Protectionist Barriers from Rich Countries

Since at least the mid-1980s, the rich countries have been part of the problem rather than part of the solution to increasing agricultural productivity in low-income countries. Agricultural protection in the OECD countries remains very high, despite agreements at the Uruguay Round of trade negotiations that brought agriculture within the purview of the WTO. This protection has two pernicious effects. First, by maintaining production levels well above those that would be profitable without the subsidies and protection, global supplies have been increased and world prices lowered. The actual consequences for developing countries have been mixed and hotly disputed, as a number of countries protect themselves against these "unfair" prices. It is entirely possible that farmers and consumers in Indonesia, for example, might face lower rice prices after market liberalization because of the high protection provided now, even at prices prevailing in late 2008.

Second, and perhaps more important, the rich countries have reserved an increasing share of world agricultural consumption for their own protected farmers. The share of rich countries in agricultural exports has actually increased significantly in the past thirty years, contradicting everything economists think they know about comparative advantage and the structural transformation. Exports from high-income countries in the late 1960s were 55 percent of global agricultural trade. That share climbed to 75 percent in the mid-1990s, before declining slowly to about 67 percent in 2005.[8] This would simply not have been possible without the massive subsidies the rich countries devote to their farmers. The impact, of course, is to take market share away from the world's poorest farmers.

There is also a disconcerting concern in the legislatures of some rich countries, and especially in the United States, that successful agricultural development in poor countries will impair the export markets for agricultural products from rich countries. This concern is manifest in legislative directives that prohibit the United States Agency for International Development (USAID), for example, from helping poor countries develop their soybean, sugar, or orange industries, and in the continued insistence that food aid is "development assistance," despite overwhelming evidence that it usually distorts market incentives for local farmers.[9] (Cash transfers of even half the nominal value of the food aid would almost certainly do more good.)

Efforts have been made over the years to build the case that agricultural development is the necessary first step for overall economic development—that developing countries quickly graduate from receiving aid to serving as commercial markets for agricultural exports. That case has strong historical precedents, and there can be little doubt that national welfare in both poor- and rich-country trading partners rises with economic growth in the poor country. But specific individual commodity producers in rich countries can also lose in this process, and these actors can be powerful advocates for restrictions on how development assistance is delivered to poor countries. By distorting public-sector support for agricultural development by the rich donors, these commodity interests also thwart more rapid economic growth and poverty reduction.

Stagnant Technology and Much More Complicated Technical Problems

Modern science and technology have wrought revolution after revolution in agriculture, resulting in crop yields and labor productivity so high in advanced countries that farmers are routinely paid to curb their abundance.[10] The Green Revolution technologies that emerged from the Consultative Group on International Agricultural Research (CGIAR) system in the 1960s provided a stimulus not just to the agricultural economies of the Asian countries able to utilize the fertilizer-responsive varieties of wheat and rice, but also to pro-poor economic growth throughout the region.

But two problems loom increasingly large. First, grain yields in Asia and Africa have been flat since the early 1990s, and the highest yielding experimental varieties at the International Rice Research Institute (IRRI) are no more productive than in 1990.[11] Unless modern genetic technologies are brought to bear on the problem, there is little promise of a radical breakthrough in the foreseeable future.[12] Still, farmers have opportunities to increase cereal yields through better management practices, even if the genetic potential of their seeds is not rising steadily.

Second, Africa's cropping systems and (lack of) water control make agricultural research there complicated and expensive. There are few uniform tracts of monocropped cereals with good water control and easy access to commercial inputs such as fertilizer—precisely the circumstances that made the Green Revolution feasible in Asia. The harsh environment, both agronomically and commercially, is one reason for the complex cropping systems and risk-averse behavior. But such cropping systems are notoriously hard to improve, because standard research methodologies seek to control all variables but the one under investigation. There are just too many variables for this approach to work very effectively in most African agricultural settings.

There have been successes.[13] Hybrid maize and sorghum work well in Africa when appropriate inputs are available, and when markets are available for the surpluses produced. High-value crops such as green beans and flowers are exported successfully to Europe. A number of tree crops thrive when infrastructure is available and border prices reach farmers. But the overall trend in food production per capita has been negative for two decades, and there is little prospect of reversing that trend without massive investment in rural infrastructure and specialized agricultural research, neither of which seems to be on government agendas. Adrian Wood's "hollowed out" African continent is not exactly a picture of pro-poor growth led by agriculture.[14]

Distracted Donors and Development Fads

The goals and mechanisms of development assistance have broadened considerably since the field was founded in the 1950s. From an early emphasis on growth in GDP and the containment of communism, the mandate of most development agencies, and especially that of USAID, grew to include, among many other things, reductions in poverty, improvements in child health, gender equity, environmental sustainability, transition to market economies, and democratization.[15]

In the early 1990s, Brian Atwood tried to sharpen USAID's increasingly blurred focus by shelving the agency's economic growth agenda and emphasizing instead several themes of great interest to Congress: short-run humanitarian assistance, especially food aid; health care, especially child survival and family planning programs; environmental sustainability, especially the development of agricultural technology for poor farmers (including women) working in fragile ecosystems; and gender issues more broadly. As the challenges and opportunities presented by the collapse of communism in the former Soviet Union became apparent, democratization was added as a USAID objective.

Partly because so many new topics are on the development agenda, and partly because there is no accepted core of development theory and only hotly contested empirical "truths," fads have long dominated donor thinking about appropriate development strategy.[16] From community development in the 1950s, to import substitution in the 1960s, to reaching the poorest of the poor by delivering basic needs in the 1970s, to structural adjustment in the 1980s, to sustainable development in the 1990s, and back to community development after the new millennium (now in the name of "community-*driven* development," or CDD), the search for something "new" as the answer to poverty has actually impeded the implementation of core strategies that focus on sound governance, effective macroeconomic management, and a reliance on sustained public support for private markets.

Somehow lost in the multiple agendas and donor efforts to program effectively in the face of developmental complexity was the need to achieve and sustain economic growth in poor countries for any viable long-term solutions to all of their broader problems. To turn on its head the title of Paul Streeten's famous book on meeting basic needs, "first things first" actually means reestablishing economic growth as the foundation of development.[17]

From the point of view of enhancing inclusive growth in developing countries—that is, linking the poor to rapid economic growth—leaders of donor agencies and managers of the global economy missed three opportunities over the past several decades. First, two decades intervened between the first and the second world food conferences with little to show in terms of increased food security and reduced poverty in the most vulnerable countries. Second, subsidies to farmers in rich countries remain extremely large, despite promises made at the Uruguay Round to reduce them significantly. Third, the Cold War and misguided development assistance took a terrible toll on good governance. Many decades have been lost in the creation of sound economic governance, and they cannot be recaptured overnight. Impatience on the part of donors will not help, and it may well impede progress.[18]

High Energy Prices and Biofuels as a "Game-Changer" for Agriculture

For many decades, rich countries have sought mechanisms to place a higher value on their agricultural sectors than market prices would indicate. Not all of the arguments for paying farmers more than the market would pay are without merit, although the most vociferous proponent governments—Japan, France, and South Korea—inevitably sound narrowly protectionist. Still, mainstream policy analysts accept—to some degree—at least three rationales for supporting agriculture in rich countries at taxpayer and consumer expense, seeing such support as appropriate public action in the face of market failures. One of these rationales is support for biofuel production as a mechanism to break dependence on imported fossil fuels and to slow emissions of greenhouse gases. Policy support for biofuels production, and the resulting impact on food prices, relates directly to the emphasis in this monograph on difficulties faced by poor countries—those still seeking a structural transformation—in providing incentives for agricultural modernization.[19] In fact, support for biofuels has the potential to reverse the historical path of structural transformation.

Biofuels are not exactly new. Although coal, the first fossil fuel, was known in China in prehistoric times and was traded in England as early as the thirteenth century, it was not used widely for industrial purposes until the seventeenth century. Until then, biofuels (such as wood and dried animal manure) were virtually the only source of energy for human economic activities, and for many poor people they remain so today. But because coal and, later, petroleum were so cheap, the widespread use of fossil fuels since the Industrial Revolution has provided a huge subsidy to these economic activities—a subsidy which seems to be nearing an end.

As fossil fuels become more expensive, what will be the role of biofuels going forward, and what will be the impact on agriculture? In the extreme, the demand for biofuels in rich countries to power their automobiles has the potential to raise the price of basic agricultural commodities to such a level that the entire structural transformation could be reversed. If so, the growing use of biofuels has two alternative futures: It could spell impoverishment for much of the world's population because of the resulting high food prices, or it could spell dynamism for rural economies and the eventual end of rural poverty. Which future turns out to be the case depends fundamentally on the technology, economics, and politics of biofuel production.[20]

The potentially devastating effects of biofuels are easy to conceptualize.[21] The income elasticity of demand for starchy staples (cereals and root crops for direct human consumption) is less than 0.2 on average, and falling with higher incomes. Adding in the indirect demand from grain-fed livestock products brings the average income elasticity to about 0.5, and this is holding steady in the face of rapid economic growth in India and China. Potential supply growth seems capable of managing this growth in demand.[22]

But the demand for biofuels is almost insatiable in relation to the base of production of staple foods. The income elasticity of demand for liquid fuels for automobile and truck fleets, not to mention power generation, is greater than 1 in developing countries. The average for the world is rising as middle-class consumers in China, India, and beyond seek to graduate from bicycles to motorbikes to automobiles. One simple calculation shows the dimension of the problem: If all the corn produced in the United States were used for ethanol to fuel automobiles, it would replace just 15 percent of current gasoline consumption in America. Something has to give.

If this were a market-driven process, it would be easy to see what would give. High grain prices would make most ethanol production uneconomical, driving down the demand for corn (and returns on investments in ethanol processing plants). Greater profitability of grain production would stimulate a supply response, although this might take several years if improved technologies were needed. Grain prices would reach a new equilibrium driven by growth in food demand from India and China, for example, with demand from the biofuel industry having only a modest impact.

This is not the scenario most analysts see. Instead, they believe, political mandates to expand biofuel production in many countries will continue to drive investor expectations and investments in processing facilities. The need to keep these facilities profitable in the face of high raw material prices will require large public subsidies. Rich countries will be able to afford these more easily than poor countries, so a combination of inelastic demand for fuel and a willingness to pay large subsidies will keep grain prices very high.

If this scenario plays out, what are the consequences for economic growth and poverty reduction in developing countries? Not surprisingly, the answer depends on the role of agriculture in the individual countries, the pattern of commodity production, and the distribution of rural assets, especially land. It is certainly possible to envision circumstances where small farmers respond to higher grain prices by increasing output and reaping higher incomes. These incomes might be spent in the local, rural nonfarm economy, stimulating investments and raising wages for nonfarm workers. In such environments, higher grain prices could stimulate an upward spiral of prosperity. After a short-run surge in the share of agriculture in GDP, caused by higher prices and greater output, the structural transformation would resume.

An alternative scenario seems more likely, however, partly because the role of small farmers has been under so much pressure in the past several decades. If only large farmers are able to reap the benefits of higher grain prices, and their profits do not stimulate a dynamic rural economy, a downward spiral can start for the poor. High food prices cut their food intake, children are sent to work instead of school, and an intergenerational poverty trap develops. If the poor are numerous enough, the entire economy is threatened, and the structural transformation comes to a halt as economic growth falters. The share of agriculture in both employment and GDP starts to rise as it becomes the sector of last resort, and this reversal condemns future generations to lower living standards.

As the historical analysis and empirical results presented in this monograph demonstrate, the structural transformation is the regular path to economic development. A reversal of the structural transformation accompanied by increased poverty would be a historic event, countering the patterns generated by market forces over the past several centuries—indeed, since the start of the era of modern economic development. Such an event would likely have stark political consequences, as populations seldom face the prospect of long-term reductions in living standards with equanimity. It is possible, of course, that new technologies will come on-stream and bring down energy costs across the board, thus allowing the biofuel dilemma to disappear quietly. But it could be a rocky couple of decades before that happens.

5

Concluding Observations

There are three basic points. First, the structural transformation has been the main pathway out of poverty for all societies, and it depends on rising productivity in *both* the agricultural and nonagricultural sectors (and the two are connected). Second, the process of structural transformation puts enormous pressure on rural societies to adjust and modernize, and these pressures are translated into visible and significant policy responses that alter agricultural prices. Third, despite the decline in relative importance of the agricultural sector, leading to the "world without agriculture" in rich societies, the process of economic growth and structural transformation requires major investments in the agricultural sector itself. This seeming paradox has complicated (and obfuscated) planning in developing countries, as well as for donor agencies seeking to speed economic growth and connect the poor to it.

This historical process of structural transformation might seem to be only a distant promise for the world's poor, who are mostly caught up in eking out a living day by day. There are many things governments can do to give them more immediate hope, such as keeping staple foods cheap and accessible and helping connect rural laborers to urban jobs. Perhaps the most valuable thing governments can do to help the poor and speed the process of structural transformation is to invest in educational and health services in rural areas. But for poverty-reducing initiatives to be feasible over long periods of time—to be "sustainable," as current development jargon would have it—the indispensable necessity is a growing economy. It is a growing economy, moreover, that successfully integrates the rural with urban sectors and stimulates

61

higher productivity in both (the investments in rural education and health help here, as well). In other words, the long-run success of poverty reduction hinges directly on a successful structural transformation.

As this monograph has emphasized, even a highly successful structural transformation is not without its problems for the poor. Two features of the structural transformation, discussed in the previous pages, give special cause for concern.

The first is a strong historical tendency toward a widening of income differences between rural and urban economies during the initial stages of the structural transformation. Even the currently rich countries saw this pattern during their development in the nineteenth and early twentieth centuries. Absolute poverty did not usually worsen during such episodes, and in East Asia the evidence is that it actually fell very rapidly during rapid structural transformation.[1] But in countries with less rapid growth, or growth that connected less well to the rural poor, the prevalence of poverty stagnated or even rose, especially in Africa.[2]

Even when absolute poverty falls, however, the widening distribution of income challenges policymakers to take corrective action. So far, the evidence is that the typical policy responses that are triggered—agricultural protection and widespread subsidies to farmers—not only fail to help the poor, but often make their fates even worse, insofar as so many of the poor must purchase their food in markets. A dynamic rural economy stimulated by real productivity growth has been pro-poor in all circumstances, but a rural economy with farm profits stimulated by protection tends to hurt the poor in both the short and long runs.

The second feature is that this tendency for the income gap between the farm and nonfarm sectors to widen during the early stages of the structural transformation is now extending much farther into the development process. Consequently, with little prospect of quickly reaching the turning point where farm and nonfarm productivity and incomes begin to converge, many poor countries are turning to agricultural protection and farm subsidies sooner rather than later in their development processes. The tendency of these actions to hurt the poor is then compounded, because the rural poor are so much more numerous in these early stages.

It is too soon to say whether the reversal of long-run downward trends in real prices of agricultural commodities—driven by demand for biofuels and possibly by the impact of climate change on agricultural productivity—will also reverse the steady movement of the turning point in the structural transformation to higher income levels. If so, the short-run impact on the poor will almost certainly be negative, but the higher real returns promised to commodity producers, without agricultural protection, could stimulate real productivity increases in rural areas, raise real wages, and be the long-run pathway out of rural poverty.

Notes

Chapter 1: The Structural Transformation in Historical Perspective

1. Clark 1940.
2. *Harvard Magazine* 2004, 57.
3. Wood 2003.
4. Maxwell 2004.
5. The causes of high food prices, especially the demand to produce biofuels using food grains and vegetable oils, are discussed briefly later in this monograph, and in detail in Timmer 2008.
6. World Bank 2004.
7. Syrquin 2006.
8. Timmer 2002.
9. Gardner 2002; Johnson 1997.
10. Gardner 2002.
11. Lindert 1991.
12. The sustainability of the production practices that generate such high levels of labor productivity in modern agriculture is the subject of intense debate (World Bank 2007; Naylor et al. 2007; Roberts 2008).
13. Lewis 1954. By modeling the flow of underemployed labor in agricultural households to more productive industrial employment and the subsequent rise of the urban industrial sector, Lewis was able to capture in a simple manner the basic elements of the structural transformation. For this and subsequent work in the field of development, he was awarded the Nobel Prize in Economics.
14. Fuglie 2004.

Chapter 2: Common Patterns and Divergent Policies, 1965–2000

1. Syrquin 1988, 212.
2. Kuznets 1955; Kuznets 1966.

3. Chenery 1960; Chenery and Taylor 1968; Chenery and Syrquin 1975.

4. Van der Meer and Yamada 1990.

5. Chenery and Taylor 1968.

6. See the technical annex to Timmer and Akkus 2008 for a list of the countries included and their representative data. All the countries had populations greater than 3 million in 2000. All of the supporting annex materials that provide econometric support for the results discussed in this monograph are available in Timmer and Akkus 2008 and its accompanying technical appendix.

7. Details of the econometric results are shown in the technical annex to Timmer and Akkus 2008, which also extracts the year and country coefficients for each Agshr variable and reports statistical and graphical results.

8. The "turning point" in all the relationships reported here is calculated by taking the first derivative of the quadratic function in lnGDPpc and setting it equal to zero. This provides meaningful estimates, of course, only when both terms of the quadratic function are significant and of opposite signs.

9. The year and country effects are extracted and shown in the technical annex to Timmer and Akkus 2008.

10. Martin and Warr 1993.

11. Some of the changes in sectoral sources of income may be definitional, in the sense that the majority source of income can switch quickly with only modest changes in actual sources of income. For example, farm workers who earn 55 percent of their income from agricultural sources (a majority) in one census year and just 45 percent (a minority) in the next will be reclassified from the agricultural to the nonagricultural labor force even though there has been only a small change in the source of their income. Such reclassifications tend to be based on census data and occur roughly every decade.

12. When the two shares are equal, labor productivity in the agricultural and nonagricultural sectors is equal—thus, potentially, income levels are equal as well.

13. See Timmer and Akkus 2008, technical annex.

14. The work by van der Meer and Yamada (1990) is an exception.

15. See the technical annex to Timmer and Akkus 2008 for details and an algebraic proof of this relationship.

16. As noted in the text, all the income data used in the analysis here are in "real" U.S. dollars, using market exchange rates and deflated to a constant 2000 basis.

17. Recall that, on average, only about 20 percent of the overall variance in the terms of trade is common to all countries on a year-to-year basis.

18. These periods might be said to correspond, respectively, with the early period of "classical" economic growth, the decade of experience with structural adjustment, and the decade when forces of globalization are thought to have taken hold.

19. Ravallion, Chen, and Sangraula 2007.

20. Olson 1965; Lindert 1991.

21. Williamson 2002.

22. Timmer and Akkus 2008.

23. Ibid., technical annex.

24. Ibid.

25. Ibid.

26. Timmer 2005b.

27. Timmer 2004; Timmer 2005a.

28. "Pro-poor growth" has been defined to mean rapid economic growth that reaches the poor in at least proportionate terms—that is, their share of economic output does not decline as average incomes rise (Besley and Cord 2006). Grimm, Klasen, and McKay (2007) review analytical issues facing the definition and implementation of pro-poor growth.

29. Krueger, Schiff, and Valdes 1991; Masters 2007; and Anderson (forthcoming).

30. Quantity effects that have an impact on food consumption are often more important for food security and nutritional well-being than price effects that are measured in markets. Such effects are not the main focus of the analysis here; see, however, Timmer 2005a for a treatment of the food security dimensions.

31. Timmer 1984.

32. Clearly, the extent to which world commodity prices are passed through into domestic economies and price formation is also a matter of domestic trade policy (and the capacity to enforce it; an early observer whose identity is long forgotten, noting the thousands of islands and small harbors close to other countries in Southeast Asia, said that "God meant Indonesia for free trade"). The technique used here to construct the domestic policy agricultural terms of trade allows for each country to have its own response to world prices.

33. An obvious concern is that domestic agricultural prices appear in some form on both sides of this regression, which should cause a *positive* bias in the estimated coefficient. But the hypothesis calls for a negative coefficient (because of how AgGAPshr is defined). Fortunately, the full statistical (fixed-effect) model has a large and significantly *negative* coefficient, so the concern over endogeneity bias is alleviated.

34. Timmer and Akkus 2008.

35. Ibid., technical annex.

36. Ibid.

37. Lindert 1991.

38. Anderson 1986.

39. Timmer and Akkus 2008, technical annex.

40. That is, the "world price" component (predicted AgToT) and the domestic policy component (domestic policy AgToT) are included separately to see their impact on the share of agriculture in employment (AgEMPshr) and the share of agriculture in GDP (AgGDPshr). The difference in the coefficients between these two regressions is then calculated as AgGAPshr to see the net effect on the structural Gini coefficient (see table 2-4).

Chapter 3: The Paradoxical Role of Agriculture in the Structural Transformation

1. This section draws on Timmer 2005b.

2. Ravallion and Huppi 1991; Ravallion and Datt 1996; Ravallion and Chen, 2007; Sumarto and Suryahadi 2003; Fan, Zhang, and Zhang 2002; Fan, Thorat, and Rao 2004; Timmer 1997; Timmer 2002; Timmer 2004; Timmer 2005a; World Bank 2007; Ravallion, Chen, and Sangraula 2007.

3. Timmer 2008.

4. Lobell et al. 2008.

5. Food and Agricultural Organization of the United Nations (FAO) 2004; Naylor and Manning 2005; World Bank 2007.

6. Johnston and Mellor 1961; Hayami and Ruttan 1985; Mundlak 2000; Timmer 2002.

7. Timmer 1988.

8. Mosher 1966.

9. Johnston and Mellor 1961.

10. Schultz 1978.

11. Johnson 1997; Gardner 2002.

12. Timmer 1988; World Bank 2004; World Bank 2007.

13. Bravo-Ortega and Lederman (2005) document clearly the different contributions of agriculture to national welfare across these various categories.

14. Lewis 1954; Johnston and Mellor 1961; Johnston and Kilby 1975.

15. Timmer 1988; Timmer 2002.

16. Byerlee 1973; Mellor and Lele 1973; King and Byerlee 1978; Hazell and Roell 1983; Haggblade, Hammer, and Hazell 1991; Hazell and Haggblade 1993; Timmer 1997; Delgado, Hopkins, and Kelly 1998; Fan, Hazell, and Thorat 2000; Fan, Zhang, and Zhang 2002; Fan, Thorat, and Rao 2004.

17. Dollar and Kraay 2002; Besley and Cord 2006.

18. Lipton 1977; Timmer 1993.

19. Dasgupta 1993.

20. Mellor 1976; Ravallion and Datt 1996; Ravallion and Chen 2007; Timmer 1997; Timmer 2002.

21. Thirtle, Lin, and Piesse 2003; Majid 2004.

22. World Bank 2007.

23. Lewis 1954.

24. Chenery and Syrquin 1975.

25. Syrquin 2006.

26. Johnston and Mellor 1961.

27. Timmer 1995.

28. Mosher 1966.

29. Prasada Rao, Maddison, and Lee 2002.

30. Mellor 1976.

31. Mellor 2000.

32. Timmer 2002.

33. Fogel 1991; Fogel 1994; Bliss and Stern 1978; Strauss 1986; Strauss and Thomas 1998.

34. Johnson 1997; Fox 2002.

35. Schultz 1993; Fogel 1991.

36. Kuznets 1955; Chenery and Syrquin 1975; Timmer 2002; World Bank 2007.

37. Timmer 1996.

38. Majid 2004.

39. Sarris 2001; Timmer 2005b.

40. Timmer 1995.

41. Lipton 1977; Timmer 1993.

42. Westphal and Robinson 2002; World Bank 2007.

43. Larson and Mundlak 1997.

44. Naylor and Falcon 1995; Elliott 2004; Elliott 2006.

45. Gardner 2002.

46. Mellor 2000; Delgado, Hopkins, and Kelly 1998; Haggblade, Hazell, and Reardon 2007.

47. Lanjouw and Lanjouw 2001.

48. Morduch 1999.

49. Zeller and Meyer 2002.

Chapter 4: Is Agricultural Development More Difficult Now? New Challenges and New Opportunities

1. A similar interpretation of the problems facing policymakers in developing countries in the 1960s and 1970s, versus the problems facing policymakers now, is put forth by Dorward et al. 2004.

2. Department for International Development (DfID) 2004.

3. Maxwell 2004.

4. Lipton 2004; Hazell et al. 2007.

5. Timmer 2008.

6. Dawe 2001; Dawe 2002; World Bank 2004; Asian Development Bank (ADB) 2008.

7. There is much talk that high food prices are here to stay, and that the new price environment will create many profitable investment opportunities for agriculture (FAO 2007; ADB 2008). A historical perspective suggests two cautionary provisos: First, in real terms, the current prices are high relative to the past several decades, but not from a longer-term perspective (Timmer 2008). Second, significant parts of the biofuel industry were uneconomic at raw material prices in mid-2008, and this reality is likely to hit home eventually among even the most enthusiastic politicians. A backlash has already started in Europe (Nonhebel 2005; Bradsher 2008; Rosenthal 2008).

8. World Bank 2008.

9. Oxfam 2002.

10. Hayami and Ruttan 1985; Johnson 1997.

11. DfID 2004.

12. Pingali, Hossai, and Gerpacio 1997; World Bank 2007.

13. Wiggins 2000; World Bank 2007.

14. Wood 2003.

15. Many institutions involved in development activities saw similar broadening of agendas. The Development Advisory Service, founded by Harvard University in the early 1960s to help poor countries prepare economic development plans, expanded its scope in 1975 to become the Harvard Institute for International Development (HIID). New activities in health, education, and rural development were integrated into the institute's traditional core of macroeconomists. The university's Women in Development program was housed in HIID. An environmental program was started in the late 1970s with the arrival of Theo Panayotou. Both in academia and government, development came to be seen as a multifaceted and complex process. This progress came at a cost, however. Focus was lost as agendas multiplied. Harvard closed HIID in June 2000, arguing that it was managerially too complex for an academic institution.

16. Easterly 2003; Sachs 2005; Collier 2007.

17. Streeten 1981.

18. Diamond 2007.

19. The two topics not dealt with at length here are support for the multiple functions performed by agriculture beyond the commodity production that is offered for sale—so-called "multifunctionality" (see Bohman et al. 1999, Losch 2004, and Tallis et al. forthcoming)—and support for "local" food systems that might offer reduced carbon footprints for most food consumers, and possibly even fresher and healthier foods (see Feenstra 2002).

20. Peskett et al. 2007.

21. Nonhebel 2002; Nonhebel 2005.

22. Naylor et al. 2007.

Chapter 5: Concluding Observations

1. Timmer 2005a.

2. World Bank 2007.

References

Anderson, Kym. 1986. Economic Growth, Structural Change and the Political Economy of Protection. In *The Political Economy of Agricultural Protection: East Asia in International Perspective,* eds. Kym Anderson and Yujiro Hayami. Allen and Unwin, Australia, 7–16.

Anderson, Kym, ed. Forthcoming. *Distortions to Agricultural Incentives: A Global Perspective.* London: Palgrave Macmillan and World Bank.

Asian Development Bank (ADB). 2008. *Special Report: Food Prices and Inflation in Developing Countries: Is Poverty Reduction Coming to an End?* Economics and Research Department, Manila, April.

Besley, Tim, and Louise Cord, eds. 2006. *Operationalizing Pro-Poor Growth: Synthesis and Country Experiences.* London: Palgrave Macmillan.

Bliss, C., and N. Stern. 1978. Productivity, Wages and Nutrition: Parts I and II. *Journal of Development Economics* 5 (4): 331–98.

Bohman, Mary, Joseph Cooper, Daniel Mullarkey, Mary Anne Normile, David Skully, Stephen Vogel, and Edwin Young. 1999. *The Use and Abuse of Multifunctionality.* Economic Research Service, U.S. Department of Agriculture, November.

Bradsher, Keith. 2008. A New, Global Oil Quandary: Costly Fuel Means Costly Calories. *New York Times,* January 19, A1 and A7.

Bravo-Ortega, Claudio, and Daniel Lederman. 2005. Agriculture and National Welfare around the World: Causality and International Heterogeneity since 1960. World Bank Policy Research Working Paper No. 3499 Washington, D.C. (February).

Byerlee, Derek. 1973. Indirect Employment and Income Distribution Effects of Agricultural Development Strategies: A Simulation Approach Applied to Nigeria. African Rural Employment Paper No. 9. Department of Agricultural Economics, Michigan State University, East Lansing, Mich.

Chenery, Hollis B. 1960. Patterns of Industrial Growth. *American Economic Review* 50 (2): 624–54.

Chenery, Hollis B., and Lance Taylor. 1968. Development Patterns among

Countries and over Time. *Review of Economics and Statistics* 50 (3): 391–416.

Chenery, Hollis B., and Moshe Syrquin. 1975. *Patterns of Development, 1950–1970.* London: Oxford University Press.

Clark, Colin. 1940. *The Conditions of Economic Progress.* London: Macmillan.

Collier, Paul. 2007. *The Bottom Billion: Why the Poorest Countries Are Failing and What Can Be Done about It.* Oxford: Oxford University Press.

Dasgupta, Partha. 1993. *An Inquiry into Well-Being and Destitution.* Oxford: Clarendon Press.

Dawe, David. 2001. How Far Down the Path to Free Trade? The Importance of Rice Price Stabilization in Developing Asia. *Food Policy* 26 (2): 163–75.

———. 2002. The Changing Structure of the World Rice Market, 1950–2000. *Food Policy* 27 (4): 355–70.

Delgado, L. Chris, J. Hopkins, and V. A. Kelly. 1998. *Agricultural Growth Linkages in Sub-Saharan Africa.* IFPRI Research Report 107. Washington, D.C.: International Food Policy Research Institute.

Department for International Development (DfID). 2004. Agriculture, Growth, and Poverty Reduction. Prepared by the Agriculture and Natural Resources Team of the UK Department for International Development, in collaboration with Anne Thomson of Oxford Policy Management, Oxford, October.

Diamond, Larry. 2007. *The Spirit of Democracy: The Struggle to Build Free Societies Throughout the World.* New York: Times Books, Henry Holt and Co.

Dollar, David, and Aart Kraay. 2002. Growth Is Good for the Poor. *Journal of Economic Growth* 7: 195–225.

Dorward, Andrew, Jonathan Kydd, Jamie Morrison, and Ian Urey. 2004. A Policy Agenda for Pro-Poor Agricultural Growth. *World Development* 32 (1): 73–89.

Easterly, William. 2003. Can Foreign Aid Buy Growth? *Journal of Economic Perspectives* 17 (2): 23–48.

Elliott, Kimberly Ann. 2004. Agricultural Protection in Rich Countries: How Did We Get Here? CGD Commentary, June 27, Center for Global Development, Washington, D.C.

———. 2006. *Delivering on Doha: Farm Trade and the Poor.* Washington, D.C.: Center for Global Development.

Fan, Shenggen, Peter Hazell, and S. K. Thorat. 2000. Government Spending, Agricultural Growth and Poverty in Rural India. *American Journal of Agricultural Economics* 82 (4): 1038–51.

Fan, Shenggen, L. Zhang, and X. Zhang. 2002. *Growth, Inequality and Poverty in Rural China: The Role of Public Investments.* IFPRI Research Report 125. Washington, D.C.: International Food Policy Research Institute.

Fan, Shenggen, S. K. Thorat, and Neetha Rao. 2004. Investment, Subsidies, and Pro-Poor Growth in Rural India. In *Institutions and Policies for Pro-Poor Agricultural Growth: Report on Project 7989,* ed. Andrew Dorward. Department for International Development (DfID) Social Science Research Unit. London, UK.

Feenstra, G. 2002. Creating Space for Sustainable Food Systems: Lessons from the Field. *Agriculture and Human Values* 19 (2): 99–106.

Fisher, A. G. B. 1935. *The Clash of Progress and Security.* London: Macmillan.

———. 1939. Production: Primary, Secondary and Tertiary. *Economic Record* 75:112–25.

Fogel, R. W. 1991. The Conquest of High Mortality and Hunger in Europe and America: Timing and Mechanisms. In *Favorites of Fortune: Technology, Growth, and Economic Development since the Industrial Revolution,* ed. P. Higonnet, D. S. Landes, and H. Rosovsky. Cambridge, Mass.: Harvard University Press.

———. 1994. Economic Growth, Population Theory, and Physiology: The Bearing of Long-Term Processes on the Making of Economic Policy. *American Economic Review* 84 (3): 369–95.

Food and Agriculture Organization of the United Nations (FAO). 2004. *State of Food and Agriculture, 2003/4: Agricultural Biotechnology: Meeting the Needs of the Poor?* Rome, Italy.

———. 2007. Despite Record 2007 Production Cereal Prices Remain High. Crop Prospects and Food Situation Report, Rome, December 6.

Fox, James W. 2002. Development Overview. Draft chapter for "Natsios Report." USAID, Washington, D.C., January.

Fuglie, Keith O. 2004. Productivity Growth in Indonesian Agriculture: 1961–2000. *Bulletin of Indonesian Economic Studies* 40 (2): 209–25.

Gardner, Bruce L. 2002. *American Agriculture in the Twentieth Century: How It Flourished and What It Cost.* Cambridge, Mass.: Harvard University Press.

Grimm, Michael, Stephan Klasen, and Andrew McKay, eds. 2007. *Determinants of Pro-Poor Growth: Analytical Issues and Findings from Country Cases.* London: Palgrave Macmillan.

Haggblade, Steven, Jeffrey Hammer, and Peter Hazell. 1991. Modeling Agricultural Growth Multipliers. *American Journal of Agricultural Economics* 73 (2): 361–74.

Haggblade, Steven, Peter B. R. Hazell, and Thomas Reardon, eds. 2007. *Transforming the Rural Nonfarm Economy: Opportunities and Threats in the Developing World*. Baltimore: Johns Hopkins University Press, for the International Food Policy Research Institute.

Harvard Magazine. 2004. John Harvard's Journal: Re-Development. November–December.

Hayami, Y., and V. Ruttan. 1985. *Agricultural Development: An International Perspective*. Revised and expanded edition. Baltimore: Johns Hopkins University Press.

Hazell, Peter, and Steven Haggblade. 1993. Farm–Nonfarm Growth Linkages and the Welfare of the Poor. In *Including the Poor: Proceedings of a Symposium Organized by the World Bank and the International Food Policy Research Institute*, ed. Michael Lipton and Jacques van der Gaag. Washington, D.C.: World Bank.

Hazell, Peter, Colin Poulton, Steve Wiggins, and Andrew Dorward. 2007. The Future of Small Farms for Poverty Reduction and Growth. IFPRI 2020 Discussion Paper 42. Washington, D.C.: International Food Policy Research Institute.

Hazell, Peter, and Ailsa Roell. 1983. *Rural Growth Linkages: Household Expenditure Patterns in Malaysia and Nigeria*. IFPRI Research Report 41. Washington, D.C.: International Food Policy Research Institute.

Johnson, D. Gale. 1997. Agriculture and the Wealth of Nations (Ely Lecture). *American Economic Review* 87 (2): 1–12.

Johnston, B. F., and J. W. Mellor. 1961. The Role of Agriculture in Economic Development. *American Economic Review* 51 (4): 566–93.

Johnston, Bruce F., and Peter Kilby. 1975. *Agriculture and Structural Transformation: Economic Strategies in Late-Developing Countries*. New York: Oxford University Press.

King, Robert P., and Derek Byerlee. 1978. Factor Intensity and Locational Impacts of Rural Consumption Patterns in Sierra Leone. *American Journal of Agricultural Economics* 60 (2): 197–206.

Krueger, Anne O., Maurice Schiff, and Alberto Valdes. 1991. *The Political Economy of Agricultural Pricing Policy*. Baltimore: Johns Hopkins University Press, for the World Bank.

Kuznets, Simon. 1955. Economic Growth and Income Inequality. *American Economic Review* 49 (1): 1–28.

———. 1966. *Modern Economic Growth*. New Haven, Conn.: Yale University Press.

Lanjouw, Jean, and Peter Lanjouw. 2001. The Rural Non-Farm Sector: Issues and Evidence from Developing Countries. *Agricultural Economics* 26 (1): 1–23.

Larson, Don, and Yair Mundlak. 1997. On the Intersectoral Migration of Agricultural Labor. *Economic Development and Cultural Change* 45 (2): 295–319.

Lewis, W. Arthur. 1954. Economic Development with Unlimited Supplies of Labor. *Manchester School* 22 (2): 139–91.

Lindert, Peter H. 1991. Historical Patterns of Agricultural Policy. In *Agriculture and the State: Growth, Employment and Poverty in Developing Countries*, ed. C. Peter Timmer. Ithaca, N.Y.: Cornell University Press.

Lipton, Michael. 1977. *Why Poor People Stay Poor: Urban Bias in World Development.* Cambridge, Mass.: Harvard University Press.

———. 2004. Launching the DfID Consultation "New Directions for Agriculture in Reducing Poverty." Department for International Development (DfID). http://dfid-agriculture-consultation.nri.org/launchpapers/simonmaxwell.html (accessed September 29, 2008).

Lobell, David B., Marshall B. Burke, Claudia Tebaldi, Michael Mastrandrea, Walter P. Falcon, and Rosamund L. Naylor. 2008. Prioritizing Climate Change Adaptation Needs for Food Security in 2030. *Science* 319 (1 February): 607–10.

Losch, Bruno. 2004. Debating the Multifunctionality of Agriculture: From Trade Negotiations to Development Policies by the South. *Journal of Agrarian Change* 4 (3): 336–60.

Majid, Nooman. 2004. Reaching Millennium Goals: How Well Does Agricultural Productivity Growth Reduce Poverty? Employment Strategy Paper 2004/12. Geneva, International Labor Organization (ILO).

Martin, Will, and Peter G. Warr. 1993. Explaining the Relative Decline of Agriculture: A Supply-Side Analysis for Indonesia. *World Bank Economic Review* 7 (3): 381–401.

Masters, Will. 2007. Past and Current Patterns of Protection in Developing Countries: General Perspective and the Case of Africa. FAO Trade and Markets Division Workshop on "Appropriate Trade Policies for Agricultural Development in a Globalizing World," Rome, December 10–11.

Maxwell, Simon, 2004. New Directions for Agriculture in Reducing Poverty: The DfID Initiative. Department for International Development. http://dfid-agriculture-consultation.nri.org/launchpapers/michaellipton.html (accessed October 1, 2008).

Mellor, John W. 1976. *The New Economics of Growth: A Strategy for India and the Developing World.* Ithaca, N.Y.: Cornell University Press.

———. 2000. Agricultural Growth, Rural Employment, and Poverty Reduction: Non-Tradables, Public Expenditure, and Balanced Growth. Report prepared for the World Bank Rural Week 2000, March.

Mellor, John W., and Uma Lele. 1973. Growth Linkages of the New Food Grain Technologies. *Indian Journal of Agricultural Economics* 18 (1): 35–55.

Morduch, Jonathan. 1999. The Microfinance Promise. *Journal of Economic Literature* 37 (4): 1569–1614.

Mosher, A. T. 1966. *Getting Agriculture Moving: Essentials for Development and Modernization.* New York: Praeger.

Mundlak, Yair. 2000. *Agriculture and Economic Growth: Theory and Measurement.* Cambridge, Mass.: Harvard University Press.

Naylor, Rosamund, and Walter P. Falcon. 1995. Is the Locus of Poverty Changing? *Food Policy* 20 (6): 501–18.

Naylor, Rosamund, and Richard Manning. 2005. Unleashing the Genius of the Genome to Feed the Developing World. *Proceedings of the American Philosophical Society* 149 (4): 515–28.

Naylor, Rosamund L., Adam J. Liska, Marshall B. Burke, Walter P. Falcon, Joanne C. Gaskell, Scott D. Rozelle, and Kenneth G. Cassman. 2007. The Ripple Effect: Biofuels, Food Security, and the Environment. *Environment: Science and Policy for Sustainable Development* 49 (9): 30–43.

Nonhebel, Sanderine. 2002. Energy Use Efficiency in Biomass Production Systems. In *Economics of Sustainable Energy Use in Agriculture*, ed. E. C. van Ierland and A. Oude Lansink. Netherlands: Kluwer Academic Publishers.

———. 2005. Renewable Energy and Food Supply: Will There Be Enough Land? *Renewable and Sustainable Energy Reviews* 9:191–201.

Olson, Mancur. 1965. *The Logic of Collective Action.* Cambridge, Mass.: Harvard University Press.

Oxfam. 2002. Boxing Match in Agricultural Trade: Will WTO Negotiations Knock Out the World's Poorest Farmers? Policy Paper 32. Oxford, U.K.: Oxfam.

Peskett, Leo, Rachel Slater, Chris Stevens, and Annie Dufey. 2007. *Biofuels, Agriculture and Poverty Reduction.* Natural Resources Perspective Series 107. Overseas Development Institute, London, June. http://www.odi.org.uk/resources/specialist/natural-resource-perspectives/107-biofuels-agriculture-poverty-reduction.pdf (accessed October 1, 2008).

Pingali, Prabhu L., Mahabub Hossain, and Roberta V. Gerpacio. 1997. *Asian Rice Bowls: The Returning Crisis?* Los Banos, Philippines: CABI Publishing, International Rice Research Institute.

Prasada Rao, D. S., Angus Maddison, and Boon Lee. 2002. International Comparison of Farm Sector Performance: Methodological Options and Empirical Findings for Asia-Pacific Economies, 1900–94. In *The Asian Economies in the Twentieth Century*, ed. Angus Maddison, D. S. Prasada Rao, and William F. Shepherd. Cheltenham, UK: Edward Elgar Publishers.

Ravallion, Martin, and Shaohua Chen. 2007. China's (Uneven) Progress against Poverty. *Journal of Development Economics* 82 (1): 1–42.

Ravallion, Martin, and G. Datt. 1996. How Important to India's Poor Is the Sectoral Composition of Economic Growth? *World Bank Economic Review* 10 (1): 1–25.

Ravallion, Martin, and Monika Huppi. 1991. "Measuring Changes in Poverty: A Methodological Case Study of Indonesia during an Adjustment Period." *World Bank Economic Review* 5 (1): 57–82.

Ravallion, Martin, Shaohua Chen, and Prem Sangraula. 2007. "New Evidence on the Urbanization of Global Poverty." Background paper for the *World Development Report 2008*. Washington, D.C.: World Bank.

Roberts, Paul. 2008. *The End of Food.* New York: Houghton-Mifflin.

Rosenthal, Elisabeth. 2008. Europe, Cutting Biofuel Subsidies, Redirects Aid to Stress Greenest Options. *New York Times*, January 19, C3.

Sachs, Jeffrey D. 2005. *The End of Poverty: Economic Possibilities for Our Times.* New York: Penguin Press

Sarris, Alexander H. 2001. "The Role of Agriculture in Economic Development and Poverty Reduction: An Empirical and Conceptual Foundation." Report prepared for the Rural Development Department of the World Bank, Washington, D.C., March.

Schultz, T. Paul. 1993. Sources of Fertility Decline in Modern Economic Growth: Is Aggregate Evidence on the Demographic Transition Credible? Unpublished paper, New Haven, Conn.: Economics Department, Yale University.

Schultz, T. W., ed. 1978. *Distortions of Agricultural Incentives.* Bloomington: Indiana University Press.

Strauss, J. 1986. Does Better Nutrition Raise Farm Productivity? *Journal of Political Economy* 94 (2): 297–320.

Strauss, J., and D. Thomas. 1998. Health, Nutrition, and Economic Development. *Journal of Economic Literature* 36 (2): 766–816.

Streeten, Paul. 1981. *First Things First: Meeting Basic Human Needs in Developing Countries.* Baltimore: Johns Hopkins University Press, for the World Bank.

Sumarto, Sudarno, and Asep Suryahadi. 2003. The Indonesian Experience on Trade Reform, Economic Growth and Poverty Reduction. Presented at the Trade, Growth and Poverty Conference (London), SMERU Research Institute, Jakarta, December 8–9.

Syrquin, Moshe. 1988. Patterns of Structural Change. In *Handbook of Development Economics*, vol. 1, eds. H. Chenery and T. N. Srinivasan. Amsterdam: North-Holland.

————. 2006. Structural Transformation. In *The Elgar Companion to Development Studies*, ed. David Alexander Clark. Cheltenham, UK: Edward Elgar Publishers.

Tallis, Heather, Peter Kareiva, Michelle Marvier, and Amy Chang. Forthcoming. An Ecosystem Services Framework to Support Both Practical Conservation and Economic Development. *Proceedings of the National Academy of Sciences*. Washington, D.C.

Thirtle, Colin, Lin Lin, and Jenifer Piesse. 2003. The Impact of Research-Led Agricultural Productivity Growth on Poverty Reduction in Africa, Asia and Latin America. *World Development* 31 (12): 1959–75.

Timmer, C. Peter. 1984. Energy and Structural Change in the Asia-Pacific Region: The Agricultural Sector. In *Energy and Structural Change in the Asia-Pacific Region: Papers and Proceedings of the Thirteenth Pacific Trade and Development Conference*, ed. Romeo M. Bautista and Seiji Naya. Manila: Philippine Institute for Development Studies and the Asian Development Bank.

————. 1988. The Agricultural Transformation. In *Handbook of Development Economics*, vol. 1, eds. H. Chenery and T.N. Srinivasan. Amsterdam: North-Holland.

————. 1993. Rural Bias in the East and Southeast Asian Rice Economy: Indonesia in Comparative Perspective. In *Beyond Urban Bias*, ed. A. Varshney. London: Frank Cass.

————. 1995. Getting Agriculture Moving: Do Markets Provide the Right Signals? *Food Policy* 20 (5): 455–72.

————. 1996. Economic Growth and Poverty Alleviation in Indonesia. In *Research in Domestic and International Agribusiness Management*, vol. 12, ed. Ray A. Goldberg. Greenwich, Conn.: JAI Press.

————. 1997. How Well Do the Poor Connect to the Growth Process? Harvard Institute for International Development for the USAID/CAER Project, December.

————. 2002. Agriculture and Economic Growth. In *Handbook of Agricultural Economics*, vol. IIA, eds. Bruce Gardner and Gordon Rausser. Amsterdam: North-Holland.

————. 2004. The Road to Pro-Poor Growth: Indonesia's Experience in Regional Perspective. *Bulletin of Indonesian Economic Studies* 40 (2): 177–207.

————. 2005a. Food Security and Economic Growth: An Asian Perspective. H. W. Arndt Memorial Lecture, Australian National University, Canberra, November 22, in *Asian-Pacific Economic Literature* 19:1–17.

————. 2005b. Agriculture and Pro-Poor Growth: An Asian Perspective. Working Paper No. 63. Center for Global Development, Washington, D.C.

————. 2008. The Causes of High Food Prices. Economics Working Paper 128, October. Asian Development Bank, Manila, the Philippines.

Timmer, C. Peter, and Selvin Akkus. 2008. The Structural Transformation as a Pathway out of Poverty: Analytics, Empirics and Politics. Working Paper No. 150 (with accompanying technical annex), Center for Global Development, Washington, D.C., available at http://cgdev.org/content/publications/detail/16421–and the technical annex–http://www.cgdev.org/doc/Working%20Papers/Technical%20Annex.pdf.

Van der Meer, Cornelis, and Saburo Yamada. 1990. *Japanese Agriculture: A Comparative Economic Analysis*. London: Routledge.

Westphal, Larry, and Sherman Robinson. 2002. *The State of Industrial Competitiveness in Developing Countries*. New York: United Nations Development Programme.

Wiggins, S. 2000. Interpreting Changes from the 1970s to the 1990s in African Agriculture through Village Studies. *World Development* 28 (4): 631–62.

Williamson, Jeffrey G. 2002. Globalization and Inequality, Past and Present. *World Bank Research Observer* 12 (2): 117–35.

Wood, Adrian. 2003. Could Africa Be Like America? In *Annual World Bank Conference on Development Economics: The New Reform Agenda*, ed. Boris Pleskovic and Nicholes Stern. New York: Oxford University Press.

World Bank. 2004. *Directions in Development: Agriculture and Poverty Reduction*. Agriculture and Rural Development Department. September.

————. 2007. *World Development Report 2008: Agriculture for Development*. London and New York: Oxford University Press.

————. 2008. *World Development Indicators, 2008*. Washington, D.C.: World Bank.

Zeller, M., and Richard I. Meyer, eds., 2002. *The Triangle of Microfinance: Financial Sustainability, Outreach and Impact*. Baltimore: Johns Hopkins University Press, for the International Food Policy Research Institute.

About the Author

Peter Timmer is a nonresident fellow at the Center for Global Development, Washington, D.C., and Thomas D. Cabot Professor of Development Studies, emeritus, Harvard University. As a faculty member at Stanford, Cornell, and Harvard universities and the University of California, San Diego, Timmer taught courses on pathways out of rural poverty, the structural transformation in historical perspective, and the role of agriculture in economic development. As a policy advisor, mostly in Indonesia, China, and Vietnam, he focused on the special nature of rice economies and the relationship between domestic markets for rice and price formation in the world market. His seminal work in the 1980s on the design and implementation of stabilization policies for rice prices in large Asian countries remains the benchmark for judging current price policies. Since early in 2007, Timmer has been deeply involved in understanding the causes of the 2007–8 world food crisis, as well as in actions at both national and international efforts to resolve it. This is a role he also played during the world food crisis of 1973–74.

The historical perspective on the structural transformation presented in the Wendt Lecture grows out of this interaction between scholarly research—understanding "why"—and policy practice—understanding "how." Timmer is convinced that successful economic transformation cannot be achieved without a policy perspective that integrates the need for long-run structural change with the short-run policies and investments needed to stimulate increases in productivity in both the rural and urban economies.

Research Staff

Gerard Alexander
Visiting Scholar

Ali Alfoneh
Visiting Research Fellow

Joseph Antos
Wilson H. Taylor Scholar in Health
Care and Retirement Policy

Leon Aron
Resident Scholar

Michael Auslin
Resident Scholar

Jeffrey Azarva
Research Fellow

Claude Barfield
Resident Scholar

Michael Barone
Resident Fellow

Roger Bate
Resident Fellow

Walter Berns
Resident Scholar

Douglas J. Besharov
Joseph J. and Violet Jacobs
Scholar in Social Welfare Studies

Andrew G. Biggs
Resident Scholar

Edward Blum
Visiting Fellow

Dan Blumenthal
Resident Fellow

John R. Bolton
Senior Fellow

Karlyn Bowman
Senior Fellow

Alex Brill
Research Fellow

Richard Burkhauser
Visiting Scholar

John E. Calfee
Resident Scholar

Charles W. Calomiris
Visiting Scholar

Lynne V. Cheney
Senior Fellow

Steven J. Davis
Visiting Scholar

Mauro De Lorenzo
Resident Fellow

Christopher DeMuth
D. C. Searle Senior Fellow

Thomas Donnelly
Resident Fellow

Nicholas Eberstadt
Henry Wendt Scholar in Political
Economy

Mark Falcoff
Resident Scholar Emeritus

John C. Fortier
Research Fellow

Ted Frank
Resident Fellow; Director, AEI Legal
Center for the Public Interest

David Frum
Resident Fellow

David Gelernter
National Fellow

Newt Gingrich
Senior Fellow

Robert A. Goldwin
Resident Scholar Emeritus

Scott Gottlieb, M.D.
Resident Fellow

Kenneth P. Green
Resident Scholar

Michael S. Greve
John G. Searle Scholar

Robert W. Hahn
Senior Fellow; Executive Director,
AEI Center for Regulatory and
Market Studies

Kevin A. Hassett
Senior Fellow; Director,
Economic Policy Studies

Steven F. Hayward
F. K. Weyerhaeuser Fellow

Robert B. Helms
Resident Scholar

Frederick M. Hess
Resident Scholar; Director,
Education Policy Studies

Ayaan Hirsi Ali
Resident Fellow

R. Glenn Hubbard
Visiting Scholar

Frederick W. Kagan
Resident Scholar

Leon R. Kass, M.D.
Hertog Fellow

Herbert G. Klein
National Fellow

Marvin H. Kosters
Resident Scholar Emeritus

Irving Kristol
Senior Fellow Emeritus

Desmond Lachman
Resident Fellow

Lee Lane
Resident Fellow

Adam Lerrick
Visiting Scholar

Philip I. Levy
Resident Scholar

James R. Lilley
Senior Fellow

Lawrence B. Lindsey
Visiting Scholar

John H. Makin
Visiting Scholar

N. Gregory Mankiw
Visiting Scholar

Aparna Mathur
Research Fellow

Lawrence M. Mead
Visiting Scholar

Allan H. Meltzer
Visiting Scholar

Thomas P. Miller
Resident Fellow

Hassan Mneimneh
Visiting Fellow

Charles Murray
W. H. Brady Scholar

Roger F. Noriega
Visiting Fellow

Michael Novak
George Frederick Jewett Scholar
in Religion, Philosophy, and
Public Policy

Norman J. Ornstein
Resident Scholar

Richard Perle
Resident Fellow

Tomas J. Philipson
Visiting Scholar

Alex J. Pollock
Resident Fellow

Vincent R. Reinhart
Resident Scholar

Michael Rubin
Resident Scholar

Sally Satel, M.D.
Resident Scholar

Gary J. Schmitt
Resident Scholar; Director,
Program on Advanced
Strategic Studies

David Schoenbrod
Visiting Scholar

Nick Schulz
DeWitt Wallace Fellow; Editor-in-Chief,
The American magazine

Joel M. Schwartz
Visiting Fellow

Kent Smetters
Visiting Scholar

Christina Hoff Sommers
Resident Scholar; Director,
W. H. Brady Program

Samuel Thernstrom
Resident Fellow; Director, AEI Press

Bill Thomas
Visiting Fellow

Richard Vedder
Visiting Scholar

Alan D. Viard
Resident Scholar

Peter J. Wallison
Arthur F. Burns Fellow in
Financial Policy Studies

David A. Weisbach
Visiting Scholar

Paul Wolfowitz
Visiting Scholar

John Yoo
Visiting Scholar